The Academy Governor

A guide to the role of governors and trustees in academies

Second edition

Adamson Publishing Ltd

Written by Stephen Adamson

The author is grateful to Phil Hand, Siddique Hussain and Michele Robbins for their kind help and advice in writing this book.

info@adamsonbooks.com
www.adamsonbooks.com

First published 2014
Second edition 2015

ISBN 978 0948543 14 2

British Library Cataloguing in Publication Data
A catalogue record for this book is available from the British Library

Cover design by Geoff Shirley

Printed by Bell and Bain Ltd, Glasgow

Contents

Introduction

Whether it was a long time ago or only last week, you probably became a governor because you wanted to make a difference, and it is pretty well certain that you also believe that the education of our children is one of the most important tasks that society must perform. It's odds on too that you have a commitment to the state system of education. And lastly, you must have felt motivated by the ethic of volunteering, because you will have realised that you were about to give up a lot of your time for little reward other than the hoped-for satisfaction of doing a good job.

The system of school governance in England and Wales is almost unique in the world in that it requires so much responsibility to be taken by non-professionals. In part this is recognition of the public nature of schools: they are both an expression of how the people of the country view our society and how we want it to develop, and a means to achieve that development. The children in it are (with the exception of the small percentage that attend private schools) the children of all of us. We regard it as important that lay people should be giving direction to the professionals who run and teach in schools, and that they hold them to account. To be suitable to perform these tasks we expect people to have the qualities that have been characterised as being behind volunteering: belief, commitment and ethics.

A lot has been spoken and written about academies, both by those who passionately believe that they are a way of moving our schools up to a higher level, and those who are sceptical about whether they bring benefits that other schools cannot. However, this can give a misleading impression that academies and maintained schools are from different families. In reality, the similarities between them considerably outweigh their differences. All the above reasons for becoming a governor apply equally to those who serve on the governing bodies of maintained schools and those on academies. If you were led blind-fold into a classroom you would probably not be able to tell whether you were in an academy or other type of state school. Similarly, the principles and the bulk of the practice of governance are the same. If you have been a governor of a maintained school before becoming one of an academy, there is a lot that will be very familiar to you.

Much, therefore, that this book will say could be transplanted to a book on maintained schools. Nevertheless, there are some distinct differences, and it is important to know what it is that is special about governing an academy, even if you have no other experience to judge by. This book endeavours to explore and explain what academy governance is about, to reveal how the different tasks cohere into a whole under one or two overarching aims, and, above all, to give practical advice on what it is that you need to do. It's not been written especially either for the person new to governance or for the old hand, but hopefully will give information and guidance that are useful to both.

No book of this size can explain everything in great detail, and if it were to try, reading it would become a mammoth task. However, it is not necessary to know everything, but merely to be aware of where specialist knowledge is required, and to be guided to where you can find it. The government website, www.gov.uk, contains much of this, and if you have the name of a document using a search engine should take you to it. But there are many other sources of useful information too. The text gives references throughout to these for readers who need the detail, and the end of each chapter lists further publications and websites that might prove useful.

If there is a substantial distinction to be found in the experiences of governance it is between primary schools and secondary schools. Those governors who have served on both often remark on this. However, the principles of governance are the same; the differences derive from the size of the institutions, the curriculum, and, of course, the behaviour patterns of the age groups of children. So while the experience might be different, the practice is the same. This book will refer at several points to what Ofsted inspectors look at when making their judgements, and it is telling that they have always examined primary and secondary schools under the same framework. A good school is one where children are taught well and learn well, know how to behave, are safe, and enjoy highly competent leadership. These should be governors' prime concerns, whatever the phase of the school.

Academy status does not cover only what are generally perceived as "academies". Free schools, University Technical Colleges and studio schools are all types of academy, with the same form of governance. The book therefore does not differentiate between them but covers all. However, there some important differences within this mix, often but not exclusively determined by whether the school became an academy voluntarily or was required to change status.

As is explained in greater depth in chapter 3, academies in multi-academy trusts have two levels of governance: the trust and the governing body, which may be called the local governing body or some other name. The body charged with legal responsibilities is the trust, but it will delegate some of these to the local level. Some of the members of a local governing body may also be members of the trust. In contrast, in standalone academies the trust is the governing body.

The distinction between trust and local governing body is not always clear cut in guidance. There are good reasons for this. The powers delegated from the trust will differ from chain to chain, so the place where a decision is made in one chain will not necessarily be the same in another. In this book we distinguish between the two bodies where it is possible to do so, in which case we refer to "the trust" and "the local governing body". Otherwise the term "the governing body" is used. Those not in standalone academies will need to familiarise themselves with the situation in their own chain.

We also generally use the term "governing body". The DfE now prefers the term "governing board". However, as this would exclusively mean "the trust" for an academy we have stuck with the more common term in order to encompass both groups, unless they can be differentiated.

Finally, the role of the clerk is an essential one in any kind of governing body, as the clerk can ensure that it works efficiently. As clerks need to understand governance, the contents of the book should be as useful to them as to governors. There is also a separate section on clerking. This should be of interest to governors too, because they need to know what it is the clerk has to do to support them, in order for them to discharge their important responsibilities well.

2. The Principles of School Governance

The governing body shall conduct the school with a view to promoting high standards of educational achievement at the school.

Education Act 2002, s. 21, page 2

The fundamental principles behind governing state-funded schools are the same, whether the school is a maintained school, academy, free school, primary, secondary or special school. They stem from the main function of a governing body, which was concisely stated in the Education Act 2002 as being "to conduct the school with a view to promoting high standards of educational achievement at the school". What this described was not new then, nor has it been altered since, but the 2002 Act clarified beyond doubt that the governing body has a directing role (to "conduct the school"), and that its abiding concern must be the quality of the education that the school provides. The 2002 Act also introduced academies.

Other things are important, such as that the children are happy, that staff feel well looked after, that the buildings are bright and cheerful, that parents are involved in the school, but none of these should be the governing body's pre-eminent concern. If in any doubt, any governor should remind themselves that schools exist primarily in order to educate children.

The three core functions of governing bodies

This simple key role produces three core functions. They are stated right at the beginning of the *Governors' Handbook*, the DfE's guide to governors' responsibilities, and are reiterated in other government publications. The *Handbook* says that school governors should focus on:

- ensuring clarity of vision, ethos and strategic direction

- holding the head teacher to account for the educational performance of the school and its pupils, and the performance management of staff

- overseeing the financial performance of the school and making sure that its money is well spent.

What each of these means in practice in academies is the subject of much of the rest of this book, but it is important at the outset to grasp its essence: that governors are responsible for the aims of the school and the strategy involved in realising them, that they oversee the work of the headteacher on the quality of education provided and that they ensure that the finances are properly and efficiently run. This is a far cry from the picture sometimes still encountered of governors worrying about the school's guttering, discussing how maths should be taught, or raising funds for a school trip.

In addition to the core function, academies have three key duties because of their status as charitable bodies:

- a duty of compliance - with company and charity law (such as providing accounts and other reports)

- a duty of prudence – to manage resources carefully and ensure solvency

- a duty of care – taking advice when dealing with legally challenging issues.

Holding to the strategic

One of the most common complaints about governors is that they get involved in detailed operational matters. There is often a strong temptation to do so, because the one follows from the other. For example, if you have set aside some money in the budget for refurbishing the school entrance, you may feel that it is a logical step then to discuss what the colour should be. Or you may understand that you need to monitor how your decisions are implemented, and that leads into putting forward ideas about the methods that should be used. Everybody has an opinion on these things, so it can be easy for a meeting to slip into a discussion about them. Sometimes headteachers/principals readily go along with this, either because it diverts attention away from more pressing matters that may be uncomfortable for them, or because they have doubts about their own judgement and this shifts the responsibility for some of the decision-making. Nevertheless, undertaking operational work is not the governors' job.

Even though it may be done with the best of intentions, straying into the operational is more than just a distraction, but can be destructive. There are two reasons why this is so. The first is explicit in the three core functions, which make it clear that the governor's role is essentially a "hands off" one. The key words used are "ensuring", "holding to account" and "overseeing", with no mention of "doing", "making" or "managing". Governors employ the "doers" and the "managers". In some categories of maintained schools they are the direct employers, in others they have employment powers delegated to them by the local authority. In academies the employers are the trustees, who, as we have seen, may be the same people as the governors, and if not may well delegate some or all employment responsibilities to local governing bodies. Governors therefore employ other people whose job it is to "do" or to manage those who "do". The first chapter of the *Handbook* says that "Governing bodies should play a strategic role and avoid routine involvement in operational matters". If governors get involved in running the school themselves they undermine those they have appointed.

They do more than this, they undermine their own position. A clue to this is in the second of the three core functions, which refers to "holding to account". Governing bodies are the accountable body for the school. This is not made quite as explicit in the current definition of their role as it was in the previous official definition, which specifically made it clear that one role was to hold the school staff to account and be held accountable itself. Nevertheless it is there in that second function, and also in a great body of literature on the role of trustees of public bodies and charities. If you take on some part of someone else's job yourself, you cannot then hold them to account for how it is done. A simple analogy would be if you employed a window cleaner at home, but washed one of the windows yourself. Even if your reason was a doubt whether the cleaner would do that window well, you cannot blame them if the glass ends up smeary.

If this happens, nobody is being held to account because you cannot hold yourself to account. Yet accountability is a key element of our system of education, and is one of the main reasons for having school governors. So, however helpful it may seem to be to get involved as governors in operational matters, the temptation must be resisted. This does not mean, however, that you should avoid giving any practical help with the school. For example, it is perfectly acceptable (and always very welcome) to help with a school trip, read to some children, or deliver some training in your area of expertise, but in doing this you are not acting in your role as a governor but as a helpful volunteer.

Moreover, not being operational doesn't mean that you will not be involved in operational matters in any way and somehow float ethereally above the school. As we will see, the strategic role involves monitoring the work being done by the leadership team, which calls on governors to check lots of things, such as the school's safeguarding and financial procedures and that proposed pay awards are justified.

These underlying principles are the same in intent as those for the trustees of any kind of charity, who are required to set the charity's strategic direction, hold the chief executive to account and ensure financial probity and efficiency. They are also the principles that underpin the governance of private schools, although the legal framework in which these operate is different. There are various forms of published guidance that explore the nature of the trustee's role, much of which is valuable to governors who wish to explore further, and which is essential to school trustees. Most of it is published by the Charity Commission (www.gov.uk/government/organisations/charity-commission). School governors have much in common with other unpaid trustees, and a lot of their way of working can be understood in the same context.

The Charity Commission points out that decisions by trustees are corporate. As a governing body you make decisions by consensus, or if necessary by taking a vote. This protects the individual from personal responsibility for any act they perform on behalf of the governing body and from any legal action taken against the governing body, providing that the individual has not done something outside of their legal powers. (This is not the same as not being accountable, and governing bodies, as we shall see, are scrutinised to see if they have been carrying out their role well.) It also imposes an obligation on all governors to support their governing body's decisions, even if they do not agree with them, spoke against them, or were not present when they were made. Any disagreements must be confined within the governing body, and it is highly destructive to criticise its decisions to outsiders or to publicly dissociate yourself from them. As with many aspects of governance, personal skills are sometimes required in how to deal with potentially tricky situations.

School governors are also like trustees of charities in that they are entrusted with money that belongs to others. With charities the money will come from donors among the public at large or, in the case of membership organisations, from members. With school governors the money comes from the government, and hence from all of us. This is an onerous charge if you reflect on it, as the money is raised from taxes, so, unlike supporters of charities, the donors have no choice whether to give or not.

Governors are therefore expected to act like other guardians of public money, and not abuse their position. Unfortunately, especially with the MPs' expenses scandal, there are plenty of examples of other people in public positions not doing this, but this is no excuse for not acting with complete honesty, nor from trying your hardest to get the best value for this money. Sometimes governors plead that they are "only volunteers", but the responsibility is as all the greater for being one. If you are not giving up your time and skills for financial reward, to put bread on your family's table, your only valid motivation must be to do the best possible job.

The Seven Principles of Public Life

The principles by which those in public life are expected to behave were formulated in response to a different scandal of MPs abusing their position for personal gain nearly two decades ago. And even though governors are unpaid volunteers they are still an important part of public life with significant responsibilities. These principles are commonly known as the Nolan Principles, after the name of the person who chaired the committee that investigated the affair, though properly they are *The Seven Principles of Public Life:*

Selflessness
Holders of public office should take decisions solely in terms of the public interest. They should not do so in order to gain financial or other material benefits for themselves, their family or their friends.

Integrity
Holders of public office should not place themselves under any financial or other obligation to outside individuals or organisations that might influence them in the performance of their official duties.

Objectivity
In carrying out public business, including making public appointments, awarding contracts or recommending individuals for rewards and benefits, holders of public office should make choices on merit.

Accountability
Holders of public office are accountable for their decisions and actions to the public and must submit themselves to whatever scrutiny is appropriate to their office.

Openness
Holders of public office should be as open as possible about all the decisions and actions that they take. They should give reasons for their decisions and restrict information only when the wider public interest clearly demands this.

Honesty
Holders of public office have a duty to declare any public interests relating to their public duties and to take steps to resolve any conflicts arising in a way that protects the public interest.

Leadership
Holders of public office should promote and support these principles by leadership and example.

In order to address the possibility of governors taking financial benefit, they are required once a year to state whether they have any interest in any business that might profit, directly or indirectly, from the school's activities. Then they must declare an interest during a meeting if an issue from which they might benefit comes up, irrespective of whether they listed the subject in their annual declaration or not. If so, the governor concerned should withdraw from the meeting while the matter is being discussed and not participate in the decision-making process. Thus if you were a director of a company that published educational books, you would declare this each year, and then withdraw from discussion of any decision that might lead to buying your company's books. This exclusion extends also to partners and close family members: if your spouse, permanent partner or son or daughter were the director of such a company, you would still need to declare the interest and withdraw.

Note that this does not prevent you from benefitting from that provision, merely from being part of the decision-making process. In the example quoted it might not be in the best interest of the school to be prevented from all dealings with your company: you may publish the physics textbook that is best for meeting the needs of your school's curriculum, and it would be an unjust shackle on the school if it were not able to buy it.

Custodianship of public money bears on the organisation of school governance in another way. You may have put yourself forward or been asked to stand as a governor because of particular skills that you can contribute, but it is also significant that you are a member of the public. The management of schools in England and Wales is very different from that in most of the rest of the world, in that the direction of publicly owned schools is given to non-professionals. It has been thought for many years that this democratic way of managing this public service has the potential to extract the best from that service, so for some time the constitution of governing bodies in maintained schools was designed to give a precise shape to public representation. Governor places were allocated according to those groups seen to be "stakeholders" in the school: parents, staff, the community, the local authority and, if the school was a faith school or a foundation school, the trust. The rules on representation have recently been relaxed for maintained schools, but even the new model is still in part shaped by the stakeholder principle.

As to some extent is the governing body of an academy. A few places on an academy governing body are still reserved for stakeholders: there has to be a minimum of one or two parents (determined by whether the academy is a converter academy or a sponsor academy), and a place is usually allocated for the principal, while the articles of association may also specify a member of staff and a representative of the local authority. The rest of the governors will either have been co-opted, or will belong to one of these stakeholder groups because at the time of formation the governing body decided to stick with the model it had when a maintained school (more detail is given on this in chapter 3). Who can be co-opted is designed to emphasise people from the public at large. There are rules preventing the governing body of an academy being stuffed with staff members or people who work for or are members of the local council. Most governors will therefore not have a personal interest in the school, but will represent the public interest.

We have concentrated here on what academies and maintained schools have in common, and indeed on what they have in common with other institutions, because what governance is meant to achieve and how governing bodies are expected to conduct themselves are the same for both categories. If you have been the governor of a maintained school that has changed status, or if you are ceasing to govern a maintained school and are moving on to an academy, you will not find that the essence of the job differs. If you have a sure grasp of the aim of governance, you won't have any problems. However, there are distinct differences in how the aims are achieved in practice, and there can be differences in the function of the governing body itself.

Further information

Education Act 2002, http://www.legislation.gov.uk/ukpga/2002/32/section/5

DfE, *Governors' Handbook*, www.gov.uk

J. Martin & A. Holt, *Joined-up Governance*, Adamson Publishing, rev. edn 2011

3. What's Special about Governing Academies?

The principles of governance are the same in academies as in maintained schools, but the governing body has greater autonomy.

DfE, *What is an academy?*

There is no such thing as a typical academy. If there were it would be a paradox, for the guiding principle of academies is individuality.

The keywords used in relation to academies are "autonomy" and "flexibility". Academies were first established as a way of turning round failing schools. They were designed to help schools where just about everything had been tried to raise standards but without success, so it was thought that if you take the school out of the system and release it from the system's rules, then it might well succeed in finding its own solutions to its problems. Teachers would not be constrained by the rules that determined the curriculum (even though they were established with the aim of producing a good education for all), and they could find innovative ways of teaching those pupils for whom the prescribed curriculum had not worked. Headteachers would be able to view the school's organisation creatively, and shake up established methods of delivery. Heads and governors could attract high-quality teachers by offering pay that exceeded the national rates. Overall, it was thought that academies might also deliver a shot of adrenalin to the whole system.

With the election of the Coalition in 2010, and even more so of the Conservatives in 2015, came the belief that all good schools would benefit from this freedom to innovate. Regulation was seen as shackling not only teachers and heads in struggling schools, but might also be holding back those who could otherwise find better ways to raise pupil standards in schools that had already proved that they were doing a good job. Although the commonly bandied-about phrase "freeing schools from local authority control" was inaccurate because local authorities had not controlled schools for 20 years, some headteachers were irked by having to meet local authority requirements on financial and other practical matters, felt they were not getting the right support from local authority advisers or considered that the National Curriculum was inadequate or skewed, so they gladly embraced the opportunity offered them to strike out on their own.

Since then this option has been extended to schools judged by Ofsted to be less than "good", if they ally themselves with a good or outstanding school. As a result the majority of secondary schools in England and a sizeable number of primaries are already academies.

Types of academy

Thus the academy principle is about being independent; indeed the definition of an academy is "a state funded independent school". Academies therefore have a built-in tendency to individuality. This individuality applies equally to the systems of governance, which can vary as much between two academies as it does between an academy and a maintained school. In fact, quite a lot of academy governing bodies have more in common with a nearby maintained school than they do with their nearest fellow academy.

Diversity has not, however, produced several thousand totally different schools. It's unlikely that it ever would, because the goals of school education remain the same whatever the school, children take the same national tests and public exams across the country (within the variety of having three main examination boards), and Ofsted inspects all state schools under a single inspection framework.

Moreover, the way that schools become academies has produced a certain amount of clumping. While schools can choose to become academies ("converter academies"), some still have academy status forced upon them ("sponsor academies"). These are the schools that are judged to be inadequate. The name derives from their having to be supported by another body. Initially this was often a business person prepared to invest their own money; now it is usually an institution that can provide the support in improving their standards that they have not found hitherto. The sponsor may be another school or a charitable trust. Many of these trusts also run other schools in an academy chain. There may be a strong degree of prescription within the chain with a uniformity of approach to all the schools in it and even a uniformity of look in such things as common school uniforms and a single template for the school websites.

You will know what kind of academy yours is, but for clarity here is the normal categorisation:

Converter academies have chosen to become academies.

Sponsor academy status is directed by the Secretary of State for Education or the local authority, usually because of poor results. Sponsor academies are supported by another institution, which might be a university, further education college, other school, or a trust that runs other academies ("chains").

Chains can be single groups where several schools are run one by one trust: multi-academy trusts (MATs). Academies may also form umbrella academy trusts where each keeps its own separate governing body but can also nominate representatives to sit on an umbrella trust to oversee the leadership and governance of the group. An umbrella trust can also include maintained schools.

Academies that do not join chains are known as single academy trusts or, commonly, as stand-alone academies.

There are also other types of academy, where the differences are not in the way that they are structured but are to do with how they were established or the nature of the education they offer:

Free schools are independent schools funded by the state that have been set up in response to parental demand. Free schools have academy status and hence the same independence. Parents, charities, businesses or groups of teachers may set them up. However, they will not run them – the schools have trusts and governing bodies.

University Technical Colleges are open to 14- to 19-year-olds, and specialise in technical qualifications. Their courses combine academic and practical studies. Each college is sponsored by a university.

Studio schools are small schools (around 300 pupils) for 14- to 19-year-olds that are designed to prepare them for the world of work. They deliver the National Curriculum but together with or in the form of enterprise-themed projects, with a strong emphasis on practical work. A studio school may be part of an existing maintained school or academy, or may be set up as a free-standing academy.

The governing body and the trust

Every academy has a trust, and every academy has a governing body. They may be the same.

However, they may also be quite distinct, and the degree of distinction varies considerably, not only between those categories of academy we have described, but within categories. In maintained schools the role of the governing body is defined in law, and the governing body is the statutory body charged with overseeing the school, including managing the budget it receives from the local authority. When talking about such powers much of the official literature refers to the "governing body" equally when discussing both maintained schools and academies. For example, the term was used throughout the first edition of *Governors' Handbook*, though with the initial rider "Unless otherwise stated, references to the role and duties of governing bodies refer to the role and duties of the primary legal entity responsible for a school's governance". Strictly speaking, in an academy this is the trust or board of directors, which has the powers and statutory status held by a governing body in a maintained school. Subsequent editions of the Handbook have provided greater clarity in the distinction between the trust and a separate governing body.

The trust of an academy is created by a company limited by guarantee (like many charitable trusts). The company has "members". These are the people who are financially responsible for the company; they are usually likened to shareholders. However, their financial commitment is only nominal, limited to a maximum of £10 per person. The members appoint most of the directors of the trust, or trustees, which may include themselves.

In converter academies that have not joined chains the trust is the governing body. The governing body of the previous maintained school will have made the decision for the school to change status, and will simply have added the new responsibilities that academy status brings to the many that it was used to exercising as a maintained school. However, a multi-academy trust has legal responsibility for several schools. It will probably delegate some of its powers but keep the core strategic function, because this is what the trust brings to the schools: a clear vision, a strong ethos, and a commitment to how the vision is realised in practice. But the trust is unlikely to be able to manage all the responsibilities that belonged to the separate governing bodies of the schools before they joined the trust. This would create a huge burden for a body that normally consists of only a handful of people, most or all of whom are likely to have many other demands on their time. As the *Governors' Handbook* says, "Unless otherwise stated, references to the governing body should be taken to refer to the entity within a maintained school or academy that is responsible for exercising governance functions – which in the case of multi-academy trusts may be the academy trust board, a local governing body, or a sub-committee responsible for discharging governance functions."

This introduces the new term "local governing body". A local governing body does not have a statutory status, and only has the powers delegated to it by the trust. Its constitution is determined by the trust and it can be dissolved at any time by the trust. Nevertheless, it will usually resemble the governing body of a maintained school, and will conduct its business in the same way, with similar agendas, committees and meeting patterns, but its powers will be less substantial. It may not even be called a "governing body" but "the academy council" or "academy committee" or some such. If you are on one of these, however, this does not mean that you don't have an important job to do, and what is said in this book still applies to you.

This is recognised by Ofsted, which comments on the effectiveness of the local governing body in its report, and which will recommend a review of how it operates should the academy and its leadership be judged less than good. If a review is recommended it should look at how the local governing body and trust work together.

While the powers of governing bodies in maintained schools are determined by a weight of statutory documents, the key documents for an academy are the Articles of Association and the Funding Agreement (see chapter 5). The Articles are drawn up at the time the academy is established. As with a charity, they determine the constitution of the organisation and the responsibilities of the members of the company. The DfE produces models to help new academies, and the term "local governing body" comes from these. Academy governors should look at their Articles of Association to find out just what powers they have.

Some confusion about the role of local governing bodies has been created by the DfE's definition of the trust's function as strategic and the local governing body's as operational. All other literature on schools emphasises that a governing body should not be operational, for the reasons stated in the previous chapter. Despite the DfE definition, this applies equally to the local governing body in a multi-academy trust. A more helpful way of describing the roles of the trustees and governors is to say that the latter will usually determine the overall strategy while the local body is responsible for overseeing how that strategy is applied in its school. Managing the school and implementing strategy is still the job of the principal and staff, while the local governing body should hold them to account for how this is done.

The local governing body will also usually take on the matters that are specific to the school: conducting the principal's appraisal, deciding the staffing structure and handling parental complaints, oversight of the budget, staff grievances and appeals and exclusions. The first of these is particularly significant, as it is a litmus test of how the trust values the local governing body (and in some cases it is done neither by the local governing body or the trustees but by a management panel). However, there are no hard and fast rules so there is no substitute for finding out exactly what powers are delegated to you.

The chair of a local governing body may be appointed by the trust, rather than elected by the other local governors. In fact, this practice was widespread at first, but more recently the larger multi-academy trusts have not all exercised this option, but now encourage or nominate a non-trust member of the local governing body to stand for the post.

What academies do that maintained schools do not

Academies have been designed to be exempt from some of the controls exercised on maintained schools. What this amounts to is greater freedom in five areas:

- the curriculum
- staffing
- allocation of school time
- premises
- admissions.

Although the distinction between academies and maintained schools is no longer as great as it was at the time that the government extended academy status, it is still significant.

The curriculum

With the exception of some special cases, maintained schools are required by law to teach the National Curriculum to all their pupils. The National Curriculum was introduced in 1988 because there was concern about the standard of courses and of teaching offered around the country. It was, and still is, intended to guarantee a high level of education for all children in all the main subjects. However, it is not the sum total of what a school teaches as there may be other subjects taught outside of the National Curriculum, and any enrichment activities provided by the school are also part of its curriculum.

Nevertheless, where a school failed to provide an adequate education despite attempts to improve it, it was thought that sticking rigidly to the National Curriculum might be a hindrance to improvement rather than an aid. The early academies were therefore exempt from having to teach it. This was not meant to create a free-for-all as these schools too were subject to inspection, one of whose focuses remained what the school was teaching and how effective it was. Consequently, early academies largely stuck to the National Curriculum, but made variations where it thought there were good reasons for doing so.

In extending academy status to good and outstanding schools the Coalition believed that imposing a rigid curriculum was also a constraint on schools that were already doing well. It thought that their teachers would benefit from being allowed to follow their own ideas about what and how they should teach. This proved attractive to a number of headteachers in early adopter schools. It is unusual, however, to encounter complete abandonment of the National Curriculum; more common is academies picking and choosing, with most of it left in place. Some even follow the whole thing quite happily. Academy trusts should choose according to what best meets their pupils' needs.

The National Curriculum has itself changed over the years and is much less prescriptive than it was. The new version that started being taught from September 2015 mainly concentrates on key principles and has fewer of the detailed strictures of what must be taught than were contained in earlier versions. Its aim is to address only the essential knowledge that children should have and leave it up to schools how to teach and supplement this. Maintained schools have in this respect become more like academies.

Staffing

In staffing matters, too, maintained schools have become more like academies, though significant differences remain.

Pay for teachers has for many years been determined by annually revised national scales which meant that teachers at the same level would receive the same pay wherever in the country they worked, with additional allowances for those in London. Teachers would start at point one on the mainscale and then progress up a point each year until they reached the top of the scale. It was only in cases of demonstrable poor performance that teachers would not receive this annual step-up. Once they had got to point 6, the top of the scale, they might in time apply to "cross the threshold" and move on to two (later three) upper pay spine points. Other scales determined the pay of those in leadership positions.

For schools that had stubbornly low levels of pupil achievement it was thought that additional incentives were needed to attract high-quality teachers and to reward those that put in a special performance. This extended logically from the exemption from the National Curriculum. If teachers might produce some particular inspiration or effort, it seemed right that they should receive extra reward. Consequently, the law on academies was framed to allow them to pay teachers whatever they liked.

This has not produced a pay free-for-all. Even if principals fancied taking on the job of working out individual pay for each of a large number of teachers, the pressure of a fixed overall budget would prevent many receiving large increases. Moreover, the pay rates in maintained schools would encourage those being paid less in an academy to move on elsewhere (which may be a result a head would want to achieve in individual cases but not as matter of course for much of the staff). Academies have therefore largely continued to pay teachers according to the national rates. Pay freedom has generally been reserved for key posts that can have the greatest effect, such as heads of department or good teachers in shortage subjects.

This may change in the coming years. Substantial changes have been made to the pay structure for all teachers, with progression up the pay ranges now being determined by performance. Maintained schools have to base their pay decisions on an annual appraisal of each teacher (more is given on this in chapter 6). In time it possible that even the pay ranges, which now determine minimum and maximum pay rates, will disappear.

Allocation of school time

All state schools are obliged to provide a minimum of 190 days' teaching for their pupils each year. To be strictly accurate, the law states that they must be open for education for 380 sessions (i.e. mornings and afternoons). Academies can determine how those days are spread around the year: the number of terms, the length of those terms, and even when the school year begins. In maintained schools the local authority decides the dates of the school terms and has to start the school year after the end of July. Recent years have seen the development of some variety in the numbers of terms in a year around the country, not all local authorities settling for the traditional three. Overall, this system has provided stability for those parents with children at different schools in the same authority.

There is greater variation among academies, where four-, five- and six-term years have developed. Research has shown that some children take a long time to recover momentum after a six-week break and slip backwards from where they were are the end of the summer term. In consequence, some academies have considerably reduced the length of the summer holiday. However, it is only a minority of academies that do change their term times: 6 percent according to a poll by Reform in March 2014.

From September 2016 school term dates in maintained schools will have been set by governing bodies, not local authorities, so in this area too academies and maintained schools will be more alike.

Premises

It should not be surprising that some of the distinctions between academies and maintained schools are being eroded. If one of the original purposes of academies was to produce some slack in the system so that effective new practices should emerge, any emerging benefits of wider application will in time come to be made available to all schools. However, there is one area where the rules have not changed, which is the ownership of premises.

The academy's trust becomes the owner of the school's land and buildings on a 125 year lease at the time the academy comes into being. Trustees and governors are responsible for keeping the premises in order and securing funds to improve them as necessary. Providing they have those funds, it is their decision what improvements are made to the buildings and how the land is used. In contrast, the land and buildings are owned by the local authority if the school is a community or voluntary controlled school, and although the local authority will work with the school, the decision on major changes to the physical fabric of the school belong with it. However, governors of voluntary aided and foundation schools that convert to academy status will feel more at home with their new situation as the premises of these are also owned by the trust or foundation – which is usually the Church in the case of voluntary aided schools.

Community, voluntary controlled and foundation schools have all their capital costs met by the local authority, which also meets most of these for voluntary aided schools. Academies apply directly to the Secretary of State for funds for their capital costs.

Admissions

The last area where academies make decisions that rest with the local authority for many maintained schools is in setting their own admissions criteria.

However, the scope for action here is limited, as there are strict rules about what criteria are and are not allowed (the School Admissions Code). An academy could not, for example, decide that it was going to admit all its pupils on ability (unless it was a grammar school that had changed to academy status), nor could it decide to become single sex without going through the same lengthy process of consultation that any other state school would have to. These rules have been established to try to achieve fairness in what is, for academies as much as for maintained schools, a publicly funded service for the public's children. For example, no state school can select on the basis of interview of the parents or pupils, nor of postcode – though it is both legitimate and very common to have proximity to the school as one of the criteria for admission. Academies are also not allowed to discriminate against children with special educational needs, those for whom English is not their first language or children on free school meals (although surveys have found that on average they have fewer such children than maintained schools). Academies, like maintained schools, also have to prioritise looked after children (children in care) and must take statemented children if so directed by the local authority.

This is not to say that the greater autonomy here is illusory. There is important scope for individual decision-making by an admissions authority. For example, it decides whether to give priority to children with siblings already in the school, how to settle which children to admit if those who all meet the existing admissions criteria exceed the number that the school can take, whether to use ability bands so as to admit equal numbers of children from each part of the ability range, or, if a faith school, how many children (up to a legal limit) to admit on the basis of their parents being adherents of the faith, and how it judges whether they really are of the faith. All the criteria need to be put into some order of priority to allow for the number of places not being equal to the eventual demand, and that is job of the admissions authority.

Again, this is an extension to academies of a power that some maintained schools already have. The admissions authority is not the local authority for all maintained schools, as voluntary aided and foundation schools are their own admissions authorities. In addition, some community and voluntary aided schools have become their own admissions authorities at the request of the local authority, although this is rare.

Autonomy always brings responsibility, and each of these five areas requires someone to make decisions. That is where the governing body and the trust come in.

Further information

Model Articles of Association, www.gov.uk

NCTL, *Governance in Multi Academy Trusts*, 2014

School Teachers' Pay and Conditions Document, www.gov.uk

School Admissions Code, www.gov.uk

4. The Educational Performance of the School and Its Pupils

Holding the head teacher to account for the educational performance of the school and its pupils…

It is only in recent years that ensuring that their school achieves high standards has become as prominent in practice as in theory for governing bodies, with a greater emphasis given to how they fulfil this role and a lesser one to their ensuring compliance with statutory regulations. Governing bodies are now very clearly held to account by Ofsted for the school's standards.

This responsibility applies both to maintained schools and academies. If anything it is, perhaps, even more pronounced with academies as local authorities are still considered to have a significant, albeit reduced, role in securing the standards of maintained schools. With academies there is no one else who can legitimately be held liable for success or failure. The buck stops with the trust and, where relevant, the governing body.

Data

It is easier to focus on this job now than it was because much more data on pupil performance has recently been made available. The key performance measures are the tests and exams taken at the ends of the two phases of most state schools: the SATs taken at the end of Key Stage 2, before pupils move on from primary schools, and the GCSEs, or vocational qualifications of comparable level, taken by students at the end of Key Stage 4, before they move on to sixth form, further education or employment. (A diminishing number of local authorities run a three-tier system with first, middle and secondary schools and a few academies fit into this structure.) For those that continue in education there are A Levels or vocational qualifications taken at the end of their school careers. ("SATs", standing for standard assessment tests, is actually an unofficial term, though universally used. In official literature they are called National Curriculum tests.)

Key Stage 1 and Key Stage 3 outcomes are also produced, but these do not attract the same attention, for reasons explained later.

The published data does not just include the results achieved in tests and exams (attainment) but also shows how pupils have progressed (achievement).

It therefore does not serve just to show where the academic high fliers are, but record what schools have done to educate all their children, whatever their educational level on entry to the school. This process of always leading pupils on from their starting point produces measures of progress referred to as "value added".

Results for all schools are public information. They are used to compile performance tables that include all maintained schools and academies so that parents, would-be parents and other members of the public can assess how well any individual school is doing. They must also be published on the school's website. Governors should be informed of these results as soon as they are available, which will be some months before the national performance tables are drawn up.

When made public, both SATs and GCSE results are published in comparative form, so that people can see not only how the school compares with others, but also how its current performance compares with its performance in recent years. This will always change to some degree, and may change very considerably. And, like the traditional warning about stocks and shares, performance can go down as well as up.

There can be many reasons behind the yearly headline figures. When there is an improvement it is common for school leaders to claim the credit for themselves and their staff. It may well be, but it is the governors' job to establish whether this is the case or not. If the results have dipped staff input is usually not given as the reason, but some other cause such as its being a poor cohort ("cohort" is simply the year group), or that the pupil make-up changed due to departures and arrivals, or, if a small school, a couple of pupils had bad days and that depressed the figures. All these may be true, or not, and again it is up to governors to probe the reasons and work out what is really happening.

It's important to note that the SATs and GCSE results that make up the performance tables that most attract publicity are only headline figures, important as they are. The significant story is in the detail, which may be masked by the aggregated figures. Pupils do not come in one size and shape, and governors need to know how different types of pupils are performing. The key factors that differentiate pupils are gender, socio-economic background, ethnicity, first language, special needs and special abilities. Accordingly, in official analyses the pupil results are broken down to show how pupils have performed according to the following groupings:

- girls and boys
- looked after children
- pupils entitled for free school meals (used as a measure of deprivation)

- stability and mobility

- ethnic group

- children for whom English is an additional language (EAL)

- children with special educational needs (SEN).

Schools are also expected to look at how they provide for gifted and talented children.

This is not, of course, a simple stratification, as all children will belong to at least one group and some will belong to two or more. However, apart from having to deal with pupil behaviour, catering for most or all of these types together represents the main challenges to teachers.

RAISEonline

A detailed report that gives data in this detail, often in several forms, is made available by Ofsted for each school. This is the RAISEonline report (Reporting and Analysis for Improvement through School self-Evaluation). It gives the overall performance of the pupils in Key Stage tests and public exams, the performance of each group, national averages for comparison, and relates the last year's results against those of the previous two years. Each school receives two versions of this each year: one in the middle of the autumn term, which provides a preliminary analysis of the previous summer's SATs or exam results (based on unvalidated data) and then several weeks later a version that incorporates any revisions once the figures have been checked (validated data). It's not necessary to wait for the validated version to study RAISEonline as it is unusual for major changes to be made, so the unvalidated version gives staff and governors a good and detailed view.

The RAISEonline report does not record information from the predecessor school, so it will not contain the data for the previous two years for an academy that has not existed that long. However, academies can still access that data so staff and governors can make the comparisons for themselves.

RAISEonline reports for primary schools also include Key Stage 1 data. This is broken down into groups in the same way as that for Key Stage 2. The information is useful as it enables governors to see progress over the seven years that most children spend in a primary school. The tests taken are not externally administered but are based on teacher assessment, with the aid of informal tests in maths, English and science. These figures are the sole measure for infant school RAISEonline reports, and correspondingly are absent from those for junior schools. Teachers also carry out formal assessments of pupils in all their subjects at the end of Key Stage 3.

The full RAISEonline report contains information about individual pupils, but there is a RAISEonline Summary Report for each school, designed for governors. To get access you need a username and password which should be provided by the school's administrator for RAISEonline, or ask to be given a pdf file of it.

School Data Dashboard

There are guides on how to use RAISEonline (see list of Further Information at the end of this chapter), but not all governors will want to scrutinise what is a long and data-rich document. It is not, anyway, necessary that they do, as a senior member of the staff, the school improvement adviser or a suitable governor should be asked to make a presentation to the governing body on its key points. One or two other governors should also read the report to corroborate, query or add to the information presented to the whole governing body. This does not mean, however, that other governors need not know and think about what the data is saying. In order to help with this Ofsted has produced a School Data Dashboard for each school, which gives the essential information in an easy-to-understand form and over just a few A4 pages (though it is made available in digital rather than paper form). This represents the minimum that each governor should know.

Ofsted does really expect governors to have absorbed what it says. Her Majesty's Chief Inspector of Schools, Sir Michael Wilshaw, made this clear when he unveiled the dashboard in February 2013:

> The School Data Dashboard I am launching today raises the stakes. Many governors know their school well already. But for those that don't, there are now no excuses. Inspectors will be very critical of governing bodies who, despite the dashboard, still don't know their school well enough.

This sounds quite threatening (and it was probably meant to be), but it is true that without knowing at least what the dashboard says you cannot carry out your prime duty of responsibility for the school's standards. This applies equally to members of the trust and those of the local governing body, even if, for the latter, the trust takes on most of the work of monitoring the school's performance.

The dashboard gives the basic information that all governors should have:

- the school's results in English and maths if a primary school and its A$\star$-C GCSEs if a secondary

- the progress made in those subjects

- the progress that should have been expected

- progress made by disadvantaged pupils compared with the others

- pupil attendance figures.

Presented in bar charts the information is for three years so that trends stand out, and a line on each chart shows the relevant national average. Under each chart is a table that shows where the school's results stand in comparison with all schools and with schools of a similar type, expressed as the national quintile (i.e. band covering 20 percent) in the which the school's results rank.

All governors should be able to understand the information. Ofsted inspectors will not only expect any governor that they meet during an inspection to know what the dashboard says about their school, but will themselves use the dashboard as a part of their pre-inspection assessment of the school.

You can look up the dashboard for any school in the country on Ofsted's website. This shows that its purpose is not only to be a tool for governors but to be a device for accountability. It enables pupils' parents, parents considering the school, teachers considering applying for posts, and others, to get a broader and more up-to-date picture of the school than that conveyed by a simple Ofsted grade at its last inspection.

The Fischer Family Trust Governor Dashboard

Fuller information is provided by another dashboard, the Fischer Family Trust Governor Dashboard. It is twice as long as Ofsted's. Produced by the Fischer Family Trust (FFT) in conjunction with the Wellcome Trust and the National Governors' Association (NGA) it is not available free to all comers. However, most academies already subscribe to the Fischer Family Trust as it provides data that is very useful for target-setting, and does some of the work of target setting for you. Schools that already subscribe to the Trust receive the dashboard for their school without further charge.

This dashboard actually uses dials, so it lives up to its name more literally than Ofsted's, though there are various graphs and charts as well. It too gives attainment in English and maths for primary schools, or A*–C GCSE passes for secondary schools. Some of the figures are also presented over three years. Where it especially adds to Ofsted is in providing information about different categories of pupil, so that governors can see whom their school is serving well and whom not so well. Thus there is a table on pupil progress for different ethnic groups, children with SEN, pupils eligible for the Pupil Premium, boys, girls and those with English as an additional language. These are put in the context of the numbers of pupils in each group, compared with national figures, so that you can see, for example, if you have a higher than average number of children with SEN.

Like the Ofsted dashboard it gives attendance figures, but it also gives performance figures for individual subjects. For primary schools these are reading, writing, maths and science, while for secondary schools they are the subjects taught at GCSE. Guides on how to use and interpret the dashboards have been produced by the FFT and the NGA and are available on their websites.

The dashboard is published early in the autumn term, using unvalidated data, and is available before RAISEonline. It is updated in January, or whenever validated data is first published.

Major changes to the National Curriculum assessment and to GCSEs taking effect from 2016 will considerably change the tools used for judging school progress. However, it will still be possible to present detailed information in data form.

Current data

Useful as all these tools are, they only provide historical information. If you are on the ball and look at what RAISEonline says in November, you are still only seeing a snapshot of the school taken six months previously.

Fortunately, schools have much more current information about how their pupils are doing these days. Indeed, it has been said that they are awash with data. All schools now have software that records pupil progress. This tracking system enables teachers to input their assessments of each child on a regular basis and then creates a record and a synthesis of what they have put in. It's still only as a good as the information that it receives, but it should be used regularly, and if teachers are not doing this it should ring alarm bells among senior management and governors. Your school staff are likely to refer to the system they use by its brand name, which is more than likely to have "tracker" or "assessment" in its title.

It would be inappropriate for governors to access the information on individual pupils themselves, but senior staff should be prepared to tell them what it says about overall progress. Thus if you have highlighted maths among children for whom the school receives Pupil Premium in year 8 as a problem, the teacher should be able to tell you instantly how they performed in the most recent class tests, how many are falling behind, and how many are running ahead.

Because the information is basically individual, with statements on each child, it can in theory be aggregated to inform you about any group of children. In addition, it will not only cover those that are in their last year in that phase of education, but those at all stages in the school. The governing body, or its Curriculum or Standards committee, should be getting current reports on a regular basis.

Testing what data says

For every bit of data, there is a narrative. Data is not an end in itself but a means of finding what that narrative is, which is basically by asking questions based on the figures you have seen. With most things in school governance, the important question that you ask is not the first one, but the follow up. So if the overall performance figures on RAISEonline are disappointing, as governors you will want to know why. When presented with the explanation, you will want a way of testing it, to see if it is true.

As we have said earlier, there are common reasons given for an apparently disappointing set of results, one of which might be that this is a poor cohort. If, for example, you are told this, the simplest thing is to ask for previous assessments of this intake. Had it been below average in each year? But even if the answer is "yes" you should want to know more about what has been done to address this. Has the school put in intervention measures to help poorly performing pupils? Are a variety of learning styles encouraged? Has the school used its Pupil Premium funding to boost children from disadvantaged backgrounds?

League tables do not just record attainment, they look at how much pupils have progressed. It's quite possible that this year's results look worse than last year's, but in fact are better. It may be that the average points score in GCSEs was worse, but the pupils had very low levels in their SATs when they started at the school. The previous year's cohort may have started at the school at a much higher point, but not have made as good progress during their time there even though they achieved more GCSE A*-Cs at the end of it.

To provide the challenge required, governors need to ask their principal for the full story behind every reason given. So if the argument is that results were depressed because a couple of pupils performed badly on the day (schools receive the marks for individual pupils), how normal is that? Any test or exam can be stressful, and it is quite normal in any group of children or adults for some to suffer from harmful nerves. Moreover, what about those who did a bit better than had been anticipated, those who pulled something out of the bag, or were lucky in the questions asked? Were there not some of them too, to redress the balance?

Perhaps there has been a high turnover of pupils. If so, then many of those pupils who sat the tests/exams were not there two years ago when the targets were set for this year's results. Moving from school to school is disrupting for children, and for many of them mobility may have an adverse affect on their performance. But there are two points to pursue here. The first is that high mobility may be a freak occurrence, but for most schools where it is a problem it is a recurring one. For example, some schools are near barracks and have a large number of pupils whose parents are in the armed services and can be moved at short notice, or they are situated in areas where asylum seekers get housed so there is always a large transient population. In which case, were there similar numbers of pupils moving around two years ago, when results were better, or did teachers not allow for the likelihood of this when setting targets? Secondly, for those "bright" children who suddenly left in the middle of the Key Stage, were not equally "bright" children received to replace them or others who left? After all, the bright children who move on are somebody's bonus input.

Another reason that is often given is that the school was unlucky in the questions asked, and that they did not address the part of the syllabus that the teachers had concentrated on. The obvious response to this is to explore why the school had not covered these parts of it. This could have been because of negligence, because teachers were diverted onto other subjects, or because they simply did not get through the syllabus fast enough. If it was genuinely a quirk of the examiners, then how were other schools affected? Are similar complaints being made more widely, and not just in this academy chain or geographical area, where there may have been a mistaken consent among teachers about what was important?

This is not to suggest that principals and teachers deliberately lie to governors. It is a quite normal human response to want to put the best gloss on bad news, especially if you feel you may be subject to criticism, and teachers are human, after all. There may also be an element of self-delusion, looking for excuses that enable us to feel better about things. There is no reason to believe that teachers are any better or worse than the rest of us in this respect.

Nor is this to suggest that governors should always be suspicious and mistrustful. It is merely that questioning is what you are told is your job: "holding the headteacher to account". It's vitally important that the system has this element in it. We don't take things at face value because nobody learns anything from that.

Finally, this is not meant to imply that governors should be rude or aggressive in their questioning, or ill-informed. The former is unnecessary, antagonises people, and is never the best way to arrive at the truth as it makes other people defensive. It's also contrary to the spirit of partnership, which is that governors and staff are working together to deliver the best to children. Being ill-informed is almost as harmful, because if you only look at half the picture and take it as the whole, you are wasting everybody's time – principal, staff and governors – and your conduct weakens the confidence that staff should have that governors know their job. This is not the same as avoiding the obvious or simple question, which can often be exactly the one that should be asked, or trying always to be clever, but means not driving home some point that is contradicted by the evidence in front of you.

A good principal will welcome the challenge and not feel undermined by it. The more accurate the picture the school has of itself, the better equipped it is to go on improving and to provide a good education. Challenging beliefs and conclusions is done to discover the real reasons behind the facts. It may well be, of course, that all those reasons given at the outset are found to be absolutely correct. If so, everyone will gain in confidence for having had them confirmed.

Working with data for improvement

Looking behind the data to discover why things turned out the way they did is only half the story, and perhaps the less important half. It's easy to become besotted with data, so it is worth keeping an eye open to make sure that none of the leadership team look like they are seduced into playing around with it all day. The sole purpose of academic data in schools is to measure teaching and learning.

Even in chains where much of the strategic work of the governing body is done for each school by the trust, the local governing body is closer to the everyday data. Trusts responsible for several academies are unlikely to have the time or opportunity to look closely at what is happening at a local level, nor to have frequent enough meetings for such information as is given to them to be up-to-date for all their schools. So even if the local governing body has no more than advisory powers, they are in this instance very important ones.

It's not the job of governors, at whatever level, to be involved in deciding what tracking software the school will use. That is an operational decision that has to be made by the staff. But governors should ask for a demonstration of the program so that teachers can show what it does and governors know what information is being made available to them. It is also right that governors should ask the critical questions at this demonstration, as this can help teachers reflect on whether the program really provides the information that they want in the form they can use, or whether there may be more things that it can deliver than they have realised.

An important aspect of challenging is monitoring. This enables challenge to be regular rather than a once- or twice-a-year exercise that comes too late to enable useful changes to be made. It's been said that governors do not monitor as such, but monitor the monitoring (David Marriott, *Monitoring and Evaluation*, third edition, 2011). This is particularly true of pupil progress. Teachers will be monitoring the progress made by the pupils in their care on a regular basis. This may be done by setting tests, looking at their work, or just noting their responses in their classroom, or probably a combination of the three. Either way, they know that in order to teach those children, they need to know what they are learning, what they are struggling with, what they find easy, and how they learn best. While up until recently test results might have been recorded on paper, now teachers will enter them into their computers so that they have a complete and regularly updated record.

As the tracking system will record marks and grades given for each child and will be able to sort them, teachers will be able to measure the progress of different groups: boys in relation to girls, different ethnic groups, those with SEN or EAL, pupils eligible for the Pupil Premium, etc.

The point of this is not just to provide interest. Governors can ask how progress is being made both overall and by these groups. For example, if history GCSE results were poor the previous year and your governing body asked the staff to take measures to improve them, you can then ask for reports that monitor whether progress is being made towards the aimed-for improvement. If yours is a primary academy and the problem was boys' reading, you can ask for information during the year to show whether the reading levels for this year's Year 6s are indeed an improvement.

These requests should not just be focused on the year groups doing the major tests and exams: year 2 for Key Stage 1, year 6 for Key Stage 2, year 9 for Key Stage 3, year 11 for GCSEs and equivalents. Pupils at all stages of the school will be tracked, and governors should be being shown information on all year groups. This enables you to discuss with the principal how the school will address weaknesses at an early stage. It's almost too late to deal with disappointing history results when the pupils get to year 11 if history has always been poor in the school. There are probably fundamental problems that need addressing, and although governors will not decide *how* they are to be addressed, they will want to know that they *are* being addressed.

You also need to know that the strategies are working. That decision that you or the trust made that history needed radical action, or that boys' reading levels were unacceptable, should have been followed up by the principal with a change, say, in the history syllabus or the adoption of a new reading scheme. You then need to know after a time whether that change is being successful, whether tracking is showing that pupils have a better grasp of the principles, facts and themes of history, and whether boys are reading more fluently. Monitoring the monitoring. And then if not, you ask the principal what is being done about it. Not every strategy is going to work, and there is nothing shameful in abandoning one that doesn't. There is, though, in persevering with it if evidence that tells you it's not working.

Even though you do not see pupils' names, given that some of the groups are very small you might be able to work out how individual children are doing. If so, you should resist the temptation to try to identify them, and if you do not even need to make an effort to guess but it is quite obvious to you, you must keep the information to yourself.

Using the Pupil Premium

One of the greatest problems in education in the UK is the very wide range of attainment across all pupils and its link to social background. Pupils from poorer families on average do much worse than those from wealthy ones. At the end of Key Stage 4 the difference is 26 percent in the number of children achieving A★–C including English and maths. The range is much greater in England than in most countries in the world, especially those that score highly in the three-yearly Programme for International Student Assessment (PISA) tests conducted by Unesco. This range is known as "the long tailback", and reducing it as "closing the gap".

A direct method of closing the gap has been with us since 2011, in the form of the Pupil Premium, a grant that provides more funds for poorer pupils. Since it was introduced, the Pupil Premium has been raised in value from its original £488 per pupil, so that in 2015 it was £1300 per annum for each eligible child in a primary school and £935 for each in a secondary school. The discrepancy between phases, which was only applied in 2014, is due to evidence that shows that the earlier social disadvantage is tackled, the better.

The money has to be spent on this group of pupils, and governors of all state schools – academies as well as maintained schools – are held to account for it. Ofsted inspectors will look at all groups of pupils when assessing whether the school provides a good education for all, but will pay particular attention to those eligible for the Pupil Premium and whether the school has succeeded in reducing the difference between their attainment and that of other pupils.

The commonly used measure for determining which pupils attract the Premium is eligibility for free school meals. The measure is not very sophisticated, and suffers from the weakness that parents have to register for their child to qualify. Although eligibility is determined by objective measures, particularly receipt of state benefits, schools do not have access to this information themselves and cannot force parents to say whether they meet the criteria or not. Nevertheless, this has long been used as the measure of deprivation as no other one until recently has been found to be pupil-specific, i.e. to be based on actual parental means, rather than statistical averages or likelihoods.

The criterion for the Pupil Premium has now been extended beyond those currently entitled to claim free school meals to those who have been eligible at any time throughout the last six years. This measure is known as "Ever 6".

The measure should be of interest to governors because a school should encourage all those parents whose children could take free school meals to register them with the school, even if they do not actually take up the meals. The school should ensure that this is done confidentially.

How the money is being used is a matter for more than interest. Governors should ensure that it is spent on those pupils it is intended for, and should get reports on how successful those actions are being. Every year the school should publish on its website:

- how much the school received in the current academic year

- how this money will be spent

- how the previous year's allocation was spent

- (most important) the outcomes of this expenditure. What difference did it make to disadvantaged pupils?

It is the responsibility of the governing body to ensure that this happens, and if inspectors call they will expect any governors they meet to know the answers to these questions.

Although the "extra" money that schools receive might be very welcome to school governors who are struggling with budgets, they must make sure that it is spent on those for whom it is intended. Governors should agree with the principal how the money is to be used, then ask for monitoring reports to ensure it has been spent as planned, and at the same time or later request evaluation of whether the expenditure has produced the results required. If it does, then the governing body will need to discuss with the principal how to build on this work, and if not it needs to ask him or her to explore alternative strategies for its use. Data on the progress being made by disadvantaged pupils will be key to the evaluation.

Governor involvement should not be at the level of detail, but should be limited to the broader issues. Governors should not be asking what support will be given to a particular pupil, but it is legitimate for them to given the strategies, such as that catch-up support is being provided in reading for pupils in Year 6.

There are various uses for the Pupil Premium that the DfE suggests, which could provide the basis of the school's report:

- one-to-one tuition: partnership interventions such as Paired Reading, not necessarily involving teachers

- peer-to-peer support, which is aimed at improving the attainment of both partners

- increasing parental involvement – evidence shows this to be a significant factor in children's learning

- professional development (CPD) to develop appropriate staff skills for working with disadvantaged children.

This list is far from exhaustive, and schools may develop their own initiatives, such as using the Premium to part-fund educational school trips, holding extension classes, or paying for teachers to run groups on Saturday mornings. The Education Endowment Foundation conducts research into what initiatives work well in helping teach children, and which ones are less successful, not just in the UK but internationally. It publishes the results in a guide for schools, *Teaching and Learning Toolkit*, which is widely consulted in making decisions about the use of the Pupil Premium. One of things the Foundation discovered is that giving effective feedback was one of the best ways of improving learning, and cost little, while reducing class sizes did not produce much benefit.

If a particular use has been tried and has not succeeded as hoped, there is nothing to be gained by trying to hide this; instead it is better for the school to see what can be learned so as to be more successful with another approach.

PE and sport

Generally academies are relatively free of regulatory requirements, but in addition to use of the Pupil Premium there is another grant about whose use primary academies, as well as maintained schools, must publish information. This is the PE and Sport Premium. This money has been made available to build on the legacy of the London Olympics, and is planned to be available up to 2020.

The PE and Sport Premium consists of a lump sum, whose amount is determined by the size of the school, and a small sum per eligible pupil, or in the case of small schools just a (larger) per pupil sum. Primary schools are to use the Premium both to increase participation in physical exercise across all children and to support achievement in sport. Each year primary schools have to publish how they have spent the grant and must include on their websites details of their sports and PE provision.

More detail is available on the education pages of Gov.uk.

Further information

Fischer Family Trust & National Governors' Association, *Governor School Performance Dashboard*, Wellcome Trust, www.fft.org.uk/fft-live/governor-dashboard.aspx

Education Endowment Foundation, *Teaching and Learning Toolkit*, http://educationendowmentfoundation.org.uk/toolkit – a summary of educational research which indicates which resources in a school are likely to be most effective in improving the attainment of disadvantaged pupils

David Marriott, *Monitoring and Evaluation*, 3rd edition, Adamson Publishing, 2011

National Governors' Association, *Knowing Your School: Primary RAISEonline* and *Knowing Your School: Secondary RAISEonline*, free to NGA members through www.nga.org.uk

PE and Sport Premium for Primary Schools, www.gov.uk

The NCTL website has a range of guidance documents for governors in www.gov.uk

5. Finance

Overseeing the financial performance of the school and making sure that its money is well spent.

The defining feature of academies is not their freedom on the curriculum, their flexibility in employing and managing staff or their control of their own admissions. It is that, as "state funded independent schools", they are funded directly by government, not via the local authority. It is significant that the document that determines how they operate and which bestows authority on them is not a commercial contract, a lease or a service agreement, but a Funding Agreement.

The Funding Agreement sets out the academy's legal obligations, the role of the governing body, the grants it will receive from the Secretary of State for Education, and its financial and accounting arrangements. It also includes the rules for terminating the academy, which are a seven-year notice by either side. Exceptions are made if the academy becomes insolvent, threatens to become insolvent or has been struck off the register of independent schools.

Members of both the trust and the local governing body should have copies of the Funding Agreement and know what it says. All trustees and especially those involved in finance should also be familiar with the *Academies Financial Handbook*, which is located on Gov.uk. The handbook is statutory guidance. It sets out the financial responsibilities of academies, and it gives more detail on most of the matters covered in this chapter.

How the budget is built

Academies receive their income stream in various packages:

- the General Annual Grant
- the Education Services Grant
- the Pupil Premium
- the Academies Capital Maintenance Fund (ACMF)
- an Earmarked Annual Grant.

The main source of money each year is the General Annual Grant (GAG), which is paid direct by the Education Funding Agency (EFA).

The GAG is intended to cover all the school's running costs. It is equivalent to the budget share that maintained schools receive, with a certain amount of top-up for expenditure that academies have to cover that would be paid for by the local authority on behalf of maintained schools. Apart from the academy's first year, when the grant is calculated on the basis of what it would have received had it remained a maintained school, the size of the grant is based on the numbers of pupils.

The Education Services Grant is also paid to local authorities and is to cover various services that local authorities provide centrally for maintained schools but which academies buy for themselves, such as school improvement, asset management and behaviour support. The grant was introduced in the school year 2013-14 to replace the Local Authority Central Spend Equivalent Grant (LACSEG), under which local authority budgets were top-sliced and the money distributed to academies to cover their additional expenditure.

Like maintained schools, academies receive the Pupil Premium for children from disadvantaged backgrounds. As this is a substantial sum (see page 37) it can amount to a large addition to the budgets for schools in deprived areas.

The school can apply for an Earmarked Annual Grant for recurrent or capital expenditure. Payment is at the discretion of the Secretary of State and is relatively rare.

The grants are calculated for each financial year, which for academies runs from 1 September to 31 August. The first instalment of the GAG is paid at the beginning of the financial year and the rest thereafter in monthly instalments.

The money received can only be spent on the purposes for which it is intended, i.e. in the case of General Annual Grant, only the education of the pupils within the school. However, a multi-academy trust (MAT) may put all the money it receives for its academies together and then allocate it as it considers best around all the schools in the trust.

Capital funding

In addition to the funds for regular running costs, academies can apply to the EFA for funding from the Academies Capital Maintenance Fund. This is available to meet significant building requirements or to replace or repair equipment whose malfunction can create health and safety hazards.

Spending the money

Expenditure as well as funding is separated into that on the normal running of the school and on capital costs. What counts as the normal running costs of an academy is defined in the Model Funding Agreement produced by the DfE as including, but not being limited to:

- teachers' salaries and related costs (including full- and part-time teaching staff and seconded teachers)

- non-teaching staff salaries and related costs (including pension contributions, educational support staff, administrative and clerical staff and manual and premises related staff)

- employees' expenses

- the purchase, maintenance, repair and replacement:

  - of teaching and learning materials and other educational equipment, including books, stationery and ICT equipment and software, sports equipment and laboratory equipment and materials

  - of other supplies and services

- examination fees

- repairs, servicing and maintenance of buildings (including redecoration, heating, plumbing, lighting, etc); maintenance of grounds (including boundary fences and walls); cleaning materials and contract cleaning; water and sewerage; fuel and light (including fuel oil, solid and other fuel, electricity and gas); rents; rates; purchase, maintenance, repairs and replacement of furniture and fittings

- insurance

- medical equipment and supplies

- staff development (including in-service training)

- curriculum development

- the costs of providing school meals for pupils (including the cost of providing free school meals to pupils who are eligible to receive them), and discretionary grants to pupils to meet the cost of pupil support, including support for pupils with special educational needs or disabilities (taking account of the fact that separate additional money will be available for pupils with statements of special educational needs)

- administration

- establishment expenses and other institutional costs.

There might appear to be an overlap between the repairs, servicing and maintenance of buildings and what the capital grant covers. The distinction is that the former is for covering ordinary on-going costs, while the capital grant is for major expenditure that represents an investment in the school.

A list of what constitutes capital expenditure is also given in the Model Funding Agreement:

- the acquisition of land and buildings

- the erection, enlargement, improvement or demolition of any building including fixed plant, installation, wall, fence or other structure, or any playground or hard standing

- the installation of electrical, mechanical or other services other than necessary replacements, repairs and maintenance due to normal wear and tear

- the purchase of vehicles and other self-propelled mechanical equipment

- the installation and equipping of premises with furnishings and equipment, other than necessary replacements, repairs and maintenance due to normal wear and tear

- the installation and equipping of premises with computers, networking for computers, operating software and information and communication technology equipment, other than necessary updates or necessary replacements, repairs and maintenance due to normal wear and tear

- the provision and equipping of premises, including playing fields and other facilities for social activities and physical recreation other than necessary replacements, repairs and maintenance due to normal wear and tear

- works of a permanent character other than the purchase or replacement of minor day-to-day items

- any major repairs or replacements which are specified as constituting capital expenditure in any grant letter relating to them

- such other items (whether of a like or dissimilar nature to any of the foregoing) of a substantial or enduring nature as the Secretary of State may agree shall constitute capital expenditure

- all professional fees properly and reasonably incurred in connection with the provision of any of the above

- VAT and other taxes payable on any of the above.

As the money will only be given for specific projects, capital expenditure is accounted for separately. Governors should monitor how this money is spent, making sure that the school is not letting expenditure overrun. For large projects it is advisable to set up a special working party or task and finish group to do this.

For the running costs of the school, governors have an ongoing responsibility, which is cyclical in nature.

Looking after the budget

Handling the budget has two aspects: setting it, and then monitoring the spend and the income. Setting the budget is a once-a-year job, although revisions may be produced at mid-year or each term. Monitoring the spend is a regular task that should be carried out at least termly.

Drawing up the budget

The amount of grant received is calculated on a per-school basis, even for academies in MATs. Their trust may simply leave the funds with each school, as it had to do anyway until 2013. If it decides to pool the budgets for all its schools and then share them out it may produce a complete budget for each school, or it may pass on responsibility for the shares to the local governing bodies for allocating into detailed budgets. This is the more likely option as the work is quite time-consuming and it would be a big job for a trust board to undertake for a number of individual schools.

Most governing bodies choose to delegate finances to a committee, although some smaller schools may handle the work in full governing body. Usually this will be called the finance committee or a resource committee, and may take on other duties that are closely related to expenditure, such as overview of the premises.

The powers that are delegated should be spelled out in terms of reference. These can include most aspects of governance of finance, but not the approval of the annual budget, which has to be given by the trust (even in the case of a multi-academy trust which has handed over budgetary matters to its individual schools). The finance committee can, however, draft it. As will be explained below, the budget is not simply a matter of allocating figures to headings, but involves decisions about the school's priorities. All governors should have been involved, and need to take ownership of the results.

There is help available with the technical side of budget-setting, which should be used. All academy trusts must employ a Chief Finance Officer (CFO), and he or she will do a lot of the detailed work. They will report to the principal or chief executive (see page 48.)

Principles of drawing up a budget

Budget-setting should be driven by the school's priorities. This might, for example, include employing more teachers to provide a broader curriculum, acquiring support to help children with special educational needs, or buying more books to help deliver the curriculum. The decisions to be made when drawing up the budget should link to the school's development/improvement plan (SD/IP), which in turn will be informed by school self-evaluation. There should be a column in the SD/IP headed "Resource", which enables the school leadership to indicate what investment is required to deliver each point. This won't necessarily be cash, as it might instead be staff time, but often it will be.

These priorities and their resource implications should be shared in advance with the CFO. This will enable him or her to draft a budget, possibly with a range of options, for you to consider when you meet. It will also counter any tendency just to make the budget the same as the previous year's with allowances for inflation, which, while time-saving, risks locking the school into a pattern that prevents it doing what it needs to do in order to improve.

The budget should be drawn up annually, before the start of the school year and as soon as possible after the amount of the GAG is known,. However, it is good practice to plan over three years. This means making assumptions about what future income will be, but is worth doing as it makes you think about the longer term, and highlights trends that might otherwise lead you into an undesired large deficit or surplus.

The approved budget must be sent to the EFA no later than 31 July each year, except for a new academy, which must submit it within four months of conversion.

Academies are not allowed to set deficit budgets, other than in exceptional circumstances, and then only with the prior consent of the Secretary of State. Nor should they produce surpluses for their own sake. Nevertheless, there are times when it is necessary to build up funds against a planned future expenditure.

Budget-setting can be a time for making tough decisions. If doing everything on your wish list costs more than the income, then you will have to decide what has to go. Although it is an option that governors are usually reluctant to use, this might include cutting staff. The governing body should already have a position on points of principle which will guide such decisions. Its view might be that it wishes to keep teachers at all costs on the basis that they are a school's principal resource, or it may value highly the contribution of teaching assistants and not want to lose any, or may even have recognised that it could be overstaffed.

The nature of school budgets

Those coming from a business background will find that schools configure their finances very differently from commercial enterprises. A major difference is that there is no concept of "profit", as schools do not exist to make money, and there are no shareholders to benefit from it if they did. Another one is that although there is plenty of choice about how you spend money, there is only a little that you can do to affect income. The main amounts received are fixed by formulae beyond the school's control. What you might be able to do is to add some through lettings, but the sums will not be large, or, as an academy, you might be able to get a grant from a trust that gives donates to charities, but these will usually be for specific projects. Alternatively, you may get financial support for a particular project from a sponsor.

The school budget should only be spent on educational purposes. One implication of this is that lettings should at least cover their costs, factoring in overtime payments to the caretaker for opening and/or closing the school and the heating and lighting costs. Another is that care should be taken in spending even small amounts on what might seem to be worthy causes like buying a gift for a member of staff who is leaving or flowers for one who has given birth.

Monitoring expenditure

When things go wrong with school finances, it is almost certainly entails a failure by governors to scrutinise expenditure properly. To help avoid this your finance committee should receive a regular statement of what the school has received and spent of the year's budget to date. This will be called something like the monthly out-turn. The fact that it is produced monthly does not mean that governors need to look at it every month, unless they have identified serious problems. Normally it is sufficient to examine the most recent one twice a term, which is typically the frequency of finance committee meetings. Detailed monitoring of the procedures is an operational matter, but the finance committee should seek evidence that the school has proper financial checks in place. Academies do not have to complete the annual Schools Financial Value Statement, but it still provides a useful checklist of questions about what governors should be doing (see Gov.uk).

The monthly out-turn will give each of the budget lines (i.e. item or group of items that produce income or incur expense, such as support staff, curriculum resources, heating). It will state the amount allocated in the budget, the amount spent/received to date, and the percentage that it represents of the budgeted amount. Crucially, it should also give a "profile", which is another percentage figure indicating the amount of the school's financial year that has elapsed. You can then assess the current figure to see whether you are on track. To give a simple example, if you were a quarter of the way through the school year, the profile would be 25%, and any percentage figure above that in the expenditure part of the report would represent a possible overspend and anything below an underspend.

However, things are not that simple, as not all money goes out in steady and regular amounts. For example, fuel bills may well not be monthly but quarterly, and they represent a major expense. Your staff may spend most of the curriculum resources money early the year, or be saving back a large part of the professional development budget for some major piece of training.

The key thing is to identify the anomalies and ask the staff why they are there. You should be prepared to probe the answer if you don't regard it as satisfactory, or ask more questions. It may also lead to making some budget revisions. For example, if the school has spent 90% of the supply cover budget by the end of the first term of the financial year, it is unlikely to get through the rest of the year without having to find more money for this budget line from somewhere else.

Because budget setting is more of an art than a science, you shouldn't expect actual expenditure to exactly follow your forecasts. It is normal to give principals some leeway to move money from one budget heading to another ("viring"), within a limit prescribed by the governing body. If, say, the school bought new IT equipment for less than planned, but wanted to buy more books to help with reading, the principal could take the saving on IT and put it into the resources budget.

Accountability

Accountability for the use of an academy's funds is shared between the principal or chief executive and the governing body or trust.

Each academy trust must appoint an accounting officer. *The Academies Financial Handbook* (2014 edition, paragraph 1.5.20) says:

> Each academy trust must designate a named individual as its accounting officer. The individual must be a fit and suitable person for the role. In trusts comprising a single school this should be the principal. In multi-academy trusts it should be the chief executive or executive principal.

Because of the need to protect public money in an organisation that is subject to little direct oversight, the role of the accounting officer goes beyond the normal duties of a principal or chief executive. *The Academies Financial Handbook* goes on:

> The role of accounting officer includes specific responsibilities for financial

matters. It includes a personal responsibility to Parliament, and to EFA's accounting officer, for the financial resources under the trust's control. Accounting Officers must be able to assure Parliament, and the public, of high standards of probity in the management of public funds.

The role has three main strands. It involves:

- ensuring that academy's money is expended and accounted for, both according to legal requirements and the stipulations of the Funding Agreement and the *Financial Handbook*

- that the way the funds are managed and accounted for is done in a proper manner

- that the academy always seeks to get value for money.

The accounting officer is required to make a written statement each year that they have met their obligations on each of these.

They are also required to inform the trust if it is considering any action that is contrary to the Handbook or the academy's own Funding Agreement. If the board, despite his/her advice, proceeds, the accounting officer must advise the EFA.

This is an accountability role and not a responsibility. The accounting officer is not expected to run the finance department themselves, but must delegate this to the CFO.

This may give the impression that the trust is let off the hook on financial matters, and that the burden is carried by the principal/chief executive. This is not the case. The trust remains responsible for agreeing a balanced budget each year and for ensuring that the funds are used lawfully and within the terms of both the Handbook and Funding Agreement. It is also responsible for the stewardship of the funds and for obtaining value for money (advice on procurement is provided by the DfE). It may look like belt and braces, and it is: the system is designed to provide double checks and secure the finances as far as is possible against misuse or fraud.

It may also seem that there is a lot of scope for confusion of roles, with trust, accounting officer and CFO all walking the same territory. To avoid this, a requirement is placed on the board of trustees to approve a written scheme of delegation that states who does what. This should reach down much further than the triumvirate of board, accounting officer and CFO to spelling out the responsibilities of the rest of the financial staff.

The board of trustees carries other financial responsibilities. It must:

- put in place internal control and risk management processes, which will define what the board considers an appropriate risk profile and determine how finances and assets are managed and overseen

- agree a business continuity plan showing how it will plan to continue in the event of a disaster

- ensure it has adequate insurance cover (the EFA offers a voluntary scheme especially for academies)

- approve accounting policies

- maintain proper accounts and prepare annual financial statements

- appoint an auditor

- receive financial reports at least once a term

- approve special items such as writing off debts

- agree a policy on receipt and donation of gifts and hospitality.

Details of all of these are given in the *Academies Financial Handbook*.

Audit

As limited liability companies, academy trusts are required to produce annual audited accounts, an obligation in charity law that is reiterated in their Funding Agreements. In the case of MATs the accounts are for the trust, not separate ones for each individual academy, though the trust is likely to ask each school to create its own accounts. The audit must be carried out by a qualified independent auditor, appointed by the board, and copies of the audited accounts must be sent to Companies House, the Secretary of State and the Principal Regulator. They must also be posted on the trust's website.

Other documents must also be prepared each year: a financial statement, a directors' report and an Accounts Return. The first two are normal procedure for charities and should be produced in accordance with the Statement of Recommended Practice (SORP) produced by the Charities Commission; the third contains key financial information, and is sent to the EFA, which uses it in compiling its own accounts. The annual accounts should be prepared according to an Accounts Direction issued by the EFA.

Members of the trust would not do the legwork on all of these, which is a job for the CFO and their staff, but must approve them.

New trusts that are not yet producing financial statements have to complete a self audit of good financial practice, the Financial Management and Governance Self-assessment (FMGS) and submit this to the EFA.

Finally, each trust should have an internal system for checking on financial controls, financial systems, transactions and risks. Larger academy trusts – defined as those with annual incomes over £50 million – must have an audit committee consisting of suitable trustees. It is left up to other trusts to decide whether they will establish a dedicated audit committee, and if not, they must instead allocate the work to another committee, such as the finance committee.

The committee does not have to do all the work itself but may commission a suitable person to do the internal audit, such as the external auditor, a bought-in internal audit service, the CFO of another academy trust or a trustee with suitable qualifications (who must not be paid for the work).

Conflicts of interest

As with all trusts, trustees and governors are required to be aware of possible conflicts of interest, and where they arise they must act in the best interests of the trust. This involves completing a register of business interests in which trustees and governors should state if they or their spouse/partner or close family members are involved in a business which might trade with the academy(ies). You should also declare any such interest should a matter arise in a meeting which might involve the business, and take no part in the discussion or the decision whether to purchase goods or services from it (see chapter 2). The trust must also publish the register of interests of trustees and members on its website.

Your business may still trade with the trust or one of its academies, but the terms must be no more favourable to the business than they would be for any other business that could have been considered.

No payment should be made to any member of the trust, or their partner or family member, unless it is permitted by the Articles of Association, and, if relevant, in agreement with the Secretary of State. Where a payment is made it must be for no more than the cost of that service. What the "cost" is may need to be defined, but the underlying principle is that no payment should be over the odds.

Financial difficulties

Academies are held to account financially by the body that provides them with their funds, the EFA. If it is concerned about how the finances of an academy trust are being managed or governed the EFA can issue a Financial Notice to Improve, and it will definitely issue one if the finances have failed. This will include a list of actions that the EFA expects the trust to take to remedy the situation. The notice automatically de-delegates the budget and the EFA manages the trust's finances until such time as it is satisfied that the trust has successfully completed the actions required of it. The situation is parallel to suspending the budget of a maintained school.

If no improvement is gained, or the financial problems are considered beyond repair, the Funding Agreement may be terminated, effectively winding up the academies in the trust.

Further information

Academies Financial Handbook on Gov.uk is the essential guide to all aspects of academy finance.

Academy funding: Information for school leaders on Gov.uk gives information on the sources of funding.

There is a range of public guidance available on public sector procurement requirements. This includes annex 4.4 of HM Treasury's *Managing Public Money*. The DfE has also produced procurement guidance: *Effective Buying for Your School*. Both are on Gov.uk.

Guidance on the funding of academies and the use of financial resources in them is also on Gov.uk, search under "academies funding".

Practical help in buying goods and services is available from the Crown Commercial Service; email education@ccs.gsi.gov.uk

6. Staffing

Holding the head teacher to account for the educational performance of the school and its pupils, and the performance management of staff.
Overseeing the financial performance of the school and making sure that its money is well spent.

Standards and staffing are closely aligned. Not surprisingly the quality of the teaching is the greatest school-led factor in pupil performance, and you won't get good educational outcomes unless the teaching is good. This is why it is normal for schools to spend well over half of their budget on teacher salaries.

Whereas once nearly all the responsibility for the quality of teaching in a school would have been placed elsewhere – the quality of initial training, the support provided by the local authority, the direction given by the head-teacher – now the governing body is held to have a significant part in de-termining it. That might sound harsh, but the accountable body for the school cannot be exempt from the most important element of the school. Although governors cannot provide good teaching themselves, nor be per-sonally equipped to tell good teaching from bad, they are expected to recog-nise the evidence of good teaching, to take steps to encourage it and to do something about it if they don't see the right signs. They also need to re-member that their staffing responsibilities do not stop at teachers – they ex-tend to all staff.

This should be familiar to governors of academies. The trust is legally the employer of the staff of a school, and much, if not nearly all, of this responsi-bility will usually be delegated in a multi-academy trust to the local governing body. This status was granted in order to give a greater freedom to academies in employing, managing and remunerating their staff.

Pay

Before academies, all state school teacher salaries were set according to na-tional, annually reviewed pay scales. These were published each year in the *School Teachers' Pay and Conditions Document* (STPCD), a fat publication which contained separate charts for the pay of ordinary teachers, experi-enced teachers, headteachers, deputies and other managers. In the first years of their careers classroom teachers would be on the mainscale, with pay determined not by their performance but by the number of years of experience they had. The expectation was that each year a teacher would move a point up the scale, unless their performance had been notably poor.

Academies have never had to follow the STPCD and can pay their teachers whatever they like. They have been enabled to use pay discretions to reward good performance, attract high fliers, fill gaps in shortage subjects, and warn teachers not pulling their weight sufficiently by not awarding any pay increase. In practice, however, most academies have followed the STPCD in deciding the pay of the majority of their teachers. This is not because pay discretion has not been welcomed, but for good reasons. If they were to pay less than maintained schools, they would quickly find that they had no teachers. If they paid more overall they would find that they had little money for everything else. The official pay scales also provide a benchmark, and are accepted across the profession. However, while the freedoms on pay have not generally been applied to each individual, they have been used to attract or reward particular teachers, mainly those in managerial positions such as heads of department, or to attract teachers to unpopular schools or those in shortage subjects.

The above paragraphs refer to the STPCD in the past tense. However, it does still exist, and remains an important document for maintained schools and a useful one for academies, but its nature has changed. The change represents another erosion of the differences between academies and maintained schools, which now have more discretion in how they reward their staff.

Governing bodies are expected to use pay as a tool in raising standards. Ofsted inspectors first looked at whether academies used them to promote good quality teaching that produced improved learning, measurable in outcomes. They expected pay to be linked to performance, with an important function filled by performance management. This approach is now equally applied to maintained schools.

Performance management

The DfE currently prefers the term "appraisal" to "performance management" but the latter will generally be used in this book as it suggests a continuous process rather a single review meeting. "Appraisal" suggests that the process is one of assuring quality, and is reactive. "Performance management" indicates that the process should be one of providing direction.

The expected link between pay and performance was made very explicit by the DfE in August 2013 when it published a revised edition of a non-statutory advice document, *Reviewing and Revising Your School's Approach to Teachers' Pay*. This stated:

Performance-related pay progression enables schools to recognise and reward a teacher's performance through an increase in pay. It can act as an incentive for continuous improvement.

Schools will already have some experience of making decisions about pay that are linked to assessments of performance – what is new is that all decisions about pay progression for teachers will need to be linked to performance in future.

The quality of the performance appraisal system in your school will be the key to this working well.

The DfE also published model pay and appraisal policies to help schools make the connection. Academies are not required by law to have policies on how they will manage pay and appraisal, but given the importance of both it is advisable all the same to have good policies, and to ensure that they are linked. If the governing body decides not to have them, then it should ensure that the principles of both are nevertheless agreed and stated, and that staff understand the factors that will apply to decisions about their pay.

There is some controversy over whether it is effective to link performance management directly with pay, but the DfE and Ofsted believe that it is and expect all schools to actively make the connection. This is what happens widely in the commercial world.

The governors' role in managing the pay and appraisal of the teaching staff is at a remove, but is direct in relation to the principal.

Performance management of the principal

Headteacher performance management has been around in schools for a number of years now, and those who served on the governing bodies of predecessor schools will be familiar with it. Although annual appraisal of the principal is not a legal requirement in academies, it is difficult to imagine the circumstances in which an academy would not think that it was necessary. The principal is the key member of staff for any academy, so the way in which he or she is performing his or her job is critical. In fact, performance management of the principal is one of the most important levers available to governors. Moreover, performance management should not just be a matter of judging how good a job the principal is doing, but one of determining the key priorities of the school for the coming year. Ofsted will look at how effectively governors use performance management.

In some MATs a number of trustees carry out the performance management of the principal themselves, or even delegate to the executive principal of the trust, rather than to the local governing body. Others will delegate to the local governing body, but will have one of the trustees on the governors' panel. This is a good indicator of the importance of the process in terms of strategy and school performance. Where this is the case the chair of the local governing body should be one of those involved in the appraisal as he or she will work closely with the principal and see the school at first hand. The whole local governing body should be informed of the objectives that have been set.

Guidance on the process for maintained schools is available in both the document already quoted from the DfE and from the NGA, and academy governors involved in the process are advised to familiarise themselves with it. The following is only a brief account of what is involved.

It is recommended that at least two governors conduct the review, and preferably three (staff governors should not take part). Training in the role is available from local authorities and may also be provided by a multi-academy trust, and unless the governors involved are very experienced in conducting performance management they should undertake this training before starting on the process.

Performance management should be an annual and planned cycle, an assessment of the previous year's performance being a part of the main review meeting, and setting new objectives in light of that assessment being the other part. The objectives are at the heart of the process. There is no limit to the number of objectives that should be set, but three or four are usually appropriate. If you set fewer it is likely that you are not covering the school's main needs, and if you set more there is a danger that there will be too many for the principal to concentrate on.

The objectives should link to the development needs of the school, and will arise from the school's self-evaluation. For example, one may be to raise the achievement of a certain group or groups of pupils who are underachieving, and another to address behaviour shortcoming or to engage more fully with parents.

The appraisal process should include discussion with the principal of their own professional development. However accomplished they are they will have some development needs: schools and the educational world move quickly so there is always something that even the hardiest professional needs to learn.

The acronym commonly used of targets is that they should be SMART – specific, measurable, achievable, relevant and time-related. Vague targets are little better than useless: "improve the performance of boys" does not highlight in what respects or give any kind of steer. They have to be measurable so that you can tell whether they have been achieved: a one percent improvement in one subject at GCSE by boys could be argued to satisfy the objective about boys, but is hardly likely to be what the governors were hoping for.

Where possible, numbers should be given. Unrealistic objectives are also useless as they merely set the person up to fail, but soft ones are not much better as they will not generate any appreciable effect. They have to be significant in terms of the school overall: setting a target that relates to only a tiny number of pupils will not achieve this. And finally, you need to indicate a date by which something is to be done or achieved.

The process is meant to be supportive as well as challenging. The DfE's guidance on appraising teachers is equally applicable to heads and principals:

> Appraisal should be a supportive, developmental process designed to ensure that all teachers have the skills and support they need to carry out their role effectively. It should help to ensure that teachers continue to improve their professional practice throughout their careers.
>
> *Reviewing and Revising Your School's Approach to Teachers' Pay*
> DfE, 2013

The review should aim for a consensus between principal and governors on the management priorities of the school, and the objectives should stem from them. The principal should agree the objectives, and indeed many principals will make their own suggestions as to what they should be, though the final decision should be the appraisers'. The review should also agree what resources are needed to achieve the objectives, whether it is deployment of staff or spending money on training, books, equipment, or whatever. Once the objectives are agreed the governors' role is not to retreat to the stands and spectate, but to engage with the principal during the year to note progress and discuss any obstacles. This should happen at least once at the mid-point of the appraisal cycle, while many schools do it termly.

You may also decide to employ an adviser for the annual review meeting. This is compulsory for maintained schools, where often a senior member of staff from the local authority is commissioned. A local governing body could use someone from the trust, or a completely independent person. An adviser with practical experience of headship, either as a current head or principal or a past one, can help the appraisers by introducing an objective view of the school and help ensure that the targets are achievable and relevant. If you use an adviser the choice should be agreed by the principal as it is important that they have confidence in the process, but avoid using one of the principal's friends or colleagues.

What has been decided must be written down. There are model forms available – from the trust, the local authority, or other schools. They include columns or boxes for the objectives themselves, success indicators, support needed, timescales, notes at the end of the year on whether met or not, and comments.

The annual appraisal ought to happen at the time that the principal's pay is due for review. Although it is not written on the form, the reviewers should make a recommendation to those who determine his or her pay on whether an increase is deserved. This will be based on whether they have met the objectives set for the year. This makes the decision-making transparent: the principal will have approved the objectives and will know that any pay progression is dependent on their meeting them. It also provides another reason for governors not to set "soft" targets, because they might otherwise find that they are rewarding performance that does not really deserve it.

When Ofsted inspectors call they will expect to be presented with good evidence of the process used to remunerate the principal according to how well he or she is doing their job. Under the old system the STPCD provided ranges for headteachers' pay according to the size of school and scales within those bands. If they met their performance objectives heads would expect to be moved up a point on the scale. The system was not always very rigorous as objectives were often not very demanding; now Ofsted will expect governors to take a more business-like approach to deciding what sort of increase to award, if any.

Performance management of teachers

Performance managing the rest of the staff is the principal's responsibility, but Ofsted requires governors to have taken steps to ensure that the process is robust and that appraisal forms the basis of pay decisions taken by the school's management.

It is logical to expect that objectives set for individual teachers line up with the school's improvement priorities, and hence with the objectives set for the headteacher. Because of the importance of this connection, you could require the principal to make these links. Naturally, there will be exceptions to this for some individuals, and in any event governors are not entitled to see the objectives set for individual teachers. Nevertheless, it means that it makes sense to carry out the headteacher's appraisal meeting before those of the other teachers.

One of Ofsted's expectations is "whether governors understand how the school makes decisions about teachers' salary progressions". You can achieve this by simply asking the principal and then looking at pupils' attainment. If the GCSE results and tracking information showed that children performed poorly in physics you would not expect to learn that teachers in this department were among the highest earners in the school (unless new staff had just been employed on advantageous terms in order to tackle the problem). Another way is for the governing body's pay panel to ask to see a range of performance review statements, anonymised, so as to judge whether pay decisions are justified.

Assuming that you have one, review the performance management policy regularly to see whether it is achieving its aims. This is best done annually, at least until your performance management and pay systems have bedded down and been seen to work well. The review should involve asking the staff for their views.

Judging the quality of teaching

You should also ask regularly about the quality of teaching. Principals should know how well each of their staff is performing his or her job. In a large school they are not able to conduct regular lesson observations of all the teachers, so this is a job to be shared with deputy and associate principals, as is performance management. It may even be devolved further, down to heads of department, but the further the devolution the more important it is to have a way of accrediting the judgements of the assessor.

Governors should know five things about their school's assessment of the quality of teaching:

- what the process of observing lessons is

- who does it

- what training they have had

- how often it happens

- how judgements are moderated.

You wouldn't expect twice termly reports, but termly would not be unreasonable. If your governing body has a Pupil Performance, Curriculum or Standards committee the report can be taken and discussed there. It is not appropriate to ask about individual teachers, and indeed doing so could compromise all the governors so that none were able to sit on any subsequent appeal committee. In small schools, though, it may be apparent who is being spoken about, in which case you will have to act as if you did not know and conceal your guesswork.

The headteacher should also give you headline figures of what the process is showing, such as 60 percent of lessons were good, 15 percent outstanding, and 25 percent requiring improvement. However, it is also relevant to ask about departments, particularly if the pupil results in the relevant subject are poor. If they are, you need to prompt the principal to find out why, to do something about it and to report back to you.

This data should then be cross-referenced to the data on progress and attainment, to show whether the judgements made relate to the outcomes. If you hear, for example, that 96 percent of the teaching in maths is good or outstanding, look at both the latest pupil results in the subject and the tracking information: if these show that performance is on a downward trend, then that would suggest that the teaching is far from good, and certainly nowhere near outstanding. You need to know what action is being taken where there are problems.

And if there are several instances where the assessments of teaching are not borne out by pupil results, then you should commission an external expert to come and do an independent assessment. This need not be presented as a threat to the principal, as a good practitioner will accept that they have limitations and look for ways to address them. But if the principal is resistant, remember that you govern the school for the benefit of the pupils, not the staff.

Performance management of support staff

Anybody employed in the school whose work is likely to impact on the children and on educational standards should have their performance reviewed. That means teaching assistants, midday supervisors, caretakers, office staff – in brief, everyone. As governors you normally do not need to know much about the process, but you should ensure that it happens.

With teaching assistants, you also need to know that they are being effectively deployed. After a great enthusiasm for employing them in the early years of the century, their value has since been questioned and some research studies have shown that pupils taken out of class for special intervention work by teaching assistants make no more progress than they would if they had simply been left with the others. Teaching assistants are not trained teachers, so they cannot be expected to provide the same level of education as the professionals. However, it has also been shown that they do contribute significantly to pupil improvement if they are well managed by their teachers, so that they are not working on their own, but are instruments for the teachers. As a report published by the Education Endowment Foundation in February 2014 says, "when used to support specific pupils in small groups or through structured interventions, Teaching Assistants can be effective at improving attainment".

The academy as employer

Staff performance and pay are only two of the employer's responsibilities that an academy has, albeit among the most challenging ones. You are also responsible for appointing staff, ensuring that the academy meets all employment legislation requirements, and deciding their working hours and their pension arrangements. Even in a small primary school academy, there is a strong case for ensuring that the school has a competent business manager who will handle most of these tasks as part of their job, apart from appointments. This may be assigned to the Chief Finance Officer. If the school budget does not run to employing a person in this role full time, then they can be employed part time or shared with a similar-sized nearby academy. In a chain this support may be provided centrally.

The actual appointment of staff should be delegated to the principal, apart from that of the principal him/herself and deputies. Deciding whom to appoint to other posts is a professional and operational decision, although individual governors may be invited by the principal to sit on an appointments panel if they have relevant skills. With one exception, the other practicalities of being an employer should also be left to professionals, providing that the governors realise that ultimately the trust is legally responsible for all employment matters. This means ensuring that the management follow health and safety procedures, procure insurance, comply with the law, and handle their own payroll. However, on one matter to do with staffing the decision resides with the governors, and that is the amount of time employees are required to work. This does not mean that they set the working hours for individual teachers, but they decided how much the school will be open across the year. All schools determine their own daily hours, but academies decide their own term lengths and times, provided that they meet the legal minimum educational provision (see chapter 3). (Maintained school governing bodies will do the same from September 2016.) The employment time for each individual employee is then a management decision, within the framework provided by the length of school terms.

When a maintained school converts to an academy the existing staff of the school come under TUPE legislation – Transfer of Undertakings (Protection of Employment). TUPE rules are quite complicated and a converting school should seek professional advice on them, but the basic principles are that staff must be re-employed by the academy under the same terms and conditions as before. In the words of ACAS:

The TUPE regulations ensure:

- that when a business transfer occurs, employees moving across to the new employer (known as the incoming employer) bring with them their length of service and terms and conditions, and

- that there is a structure for the transfer process.

Accordingly, you cannot just arbitrarily give all staff worse terms of employment on the grounds that the academy is a separate entity from the school that it replaces (although it is). If some staff are not required by the academy, their employment will have to be terminated according to whatever arrangements the predecessor school had in place for redundancy.

Pensions are subject to special arrangements. Teachers from maintained schools will normally be in the Teachers' Pension Scheme. Academies are obliged to maintain them in this scheme and to pay the employer's contributions. New teachers should also be enrolled in the scheme, unless they choose to opt out. For support staff the occupational pension scheme is the Local Government Pension Scheme (LGPS), and the academy is likewise required to make contributions to it and to offer the scheme to all new staff. There are some differences between the two schemes which means that the LGPS may be in deficit, in which case the academy becomes liable for the debt, and, depending on the staff profile of those transferring, an academy may have to pay more per member than the LA did.

Appointment of a principal

Anyone experienced in being the trustee of a charity or other third-sector organisation will be familiar with the system whereby the one appointment that the trust takes to its heart is that of the chief executive. This task meets the overriding responsibility of a trust for the strategic direction of the organisation. It's not only that the choice of a person is going to affect how the organisation develops, but that having to make that appointment allows the trustees to reflect on the nature and future needs of the organisation and shape the job according to their perceptions. The situation is directly parallel to that of a school, where the job of appointing a new headteacher/principal is normally regarded as the most important task that the governors/trustees ever perform.

It is hardly surprising, therefore, that, although they can delegate staffing responsibilities as they wish, trustees of multi-academy trusts often do not delegate this one to local governing bodies. Where they do, they may appoint an adviser to help and guide them. Standalone academies may wish to appoint a professional adviser anyway. The local authority can usually help, and will have people who guide governing bodies of maintained schools through the process. The adviser should provide knowledge of what a principal's job entails, suggest the shape of the interviews, help with finding good interview questions to ask, and be on hand to answer questions during the final discussions. However, they should not try to influence your choice; it has to be your decision whom to appoint, and no one else's.

Every appointments panel must have someone on it who has completed safeguarding training in recruitment. Until September 2014 it was validated by an official Safer Recruitment Certificate. This is no longer required, but it is still necessary for someone to have undergone appropriate training. The principal and other senior leaders will normally have done this and therefore meet the legal requirements in other staff appointments, but as the principal most definitely should not be involved in appointing his or her successor, this means that a governor has to meet the requirement. The training can be done face to face (local authorities have it as a regular feature of their governor training programmes) or on-line. There should always be at least one governor who has completed the training on every governing body, as you don't want to have to suddenly try to fit training in when you know that the principal is leaving.

Detailed guidance on the recruitment process to be followed and conducting the interview is available from the National College of Teaching and Leadership. It includes sample job descriptions, person specifications, advertisements, recruitment packs and interview questions.

Discipline and appeals

In an ideal school, every member of staff knows what their job is, is motivated and fulfilled, feels well rewarded for what they do, and knows where to go for a just solution to any problems they have. In an ideal school. But however well a school is managed and governed there are going to be times when there are staffing problems that have to be addressed.

All schools have to have procedures for addressing staff disciplinary issues, staff misconduct or staff grievances. These must be agreed by the governing body, although a multi-academy trust may do the job itself for use by all its schools. Alternatively an academy may delegate approval of the procedures to a committee or individual, including the principal. However, although this may work well for detailed scrutiny of the procedures, every governor ought to know what the final documents contain and how to deal with staffing issues.

Some accusations against staff are so serious – usually those that involve allegations of abuse of children – that the member of staff cannot remain on the premises while the allegations are investigated. In such case the person has to be suspended. The decision to do this will be the principal's, unless the person involved is the principal, in which case the decision and the handling of the procedure rests with the chair of governors. Governing bodies must also have an agreed statement of procedures for dealing with allegations of abuse made against staff. The procedures will spell out exactly what has to be done if this happens, including who has to be informed. The procedures are designed to protect staff as well as to ensure just process, as the accusations may not be true and the person could be guiltless.

But whether the complaint, allegation or grievance is very serious or relatively less so, it is important that it is handled fairly and without prejudice, and is seen to be so. For one thing, if it is not your school may well end up in an industrial tribunal, and if the ruling is against you it will cost the school a lot of money, which will have to come out of its budget. So if you don't have good procedures you are at risk of letting down not only staff but also pupils and future pupils.

Fortunately there are well established ways of handling these issues. Except where the headteacher is the subject – when the complaint should go to the chair – in no case should the governing body be involved in the first stage of handling a staffing issue. Whether it is possible lack of capability in a teacher (i.e. the quality of their teaching), a teacher acting inappropriately, or a teacher questioning a decision made about his or her pay, the matter is an operational one and for the school's management to deal with it. It is only if no outcome can be achieved that is satisfactory to both sides that governors get involved.

Your governing body needs to set up a panel to hear a grievance from a staff member or to rule on an appeal by a member of staff against dismissal. The panel usually consists of three people: an odd number ensures a majority decision can be achieved while having lots of members is impractical. For maintained schools this is a statutory provision, and it gives a good framework for academies to follow. The power of dismissal is held by the maintained school governing body, but can be delegated to the headteacher. Where it is not, the initial dismissal decision is also made by a panel of governors, in response to a recommendation from the headteacher. Some governing bodies of converter academies may have inherited this system, so it is important for the principal to check when considering dismissing a member of staff. Where there is an initial panel and then an appeal panel, the members of the two panels must be quite separate, and the members of the appeals panel must not know any details of the dismissal beforehand, other than that it has been decided on.

The governing body can have standing appeals and grievance panels by dint of electing governors to them at the start of the school year. It is also common not to do this but instead to appoint a panel, or ask for volunteers, when a case arises. The former has the advantage of establishing people at the outset so you don't have to look around at short notice. On the other hand, in many schools it is rare to need such panels, and to appoint people to them at the same time as other jobs are being shared out seems an unnecessary task. It is also argued that appointing people at the beginning of the academic year need not be much of a help because it doesn't guarantee their availability when called upon, perhaps several months later.

If the issue is one of staff misconduct it should be handled by the management and will only come to governors if it leads to dismissal or if the staff member raises a complaint under the grievance procedure. If the misconduct is regarded as severe, dismissal may not be the end of the matter as it may be referred to the National College for Teaching and Leadership to decide whether to hold a hearing into whether the teacher should be totally barred from the profession.

Further information

Guidance is available on Gov.uk for maintained schools that academy governors may find useful, especially *Managing Staff Employment in Schools* and *Implementing Your School's Approach to Pay: Departmental advice for maintained schools and local authorities*, 2014

School Teachers' Pay and Conditions Document, on the Gov.uk website

DfE, *Keeping Children Safe in Education: For schools and colleges,* www.gov.uk

DfE, David Eddy Spicer *et al.*, *Effectively Managing Headteacher Performance,* NCTL/DfE, 2014

Education Endowment Foundation, "Teaching Assistants Can Improve Literacy and Numeracy Skills When Used Effectively", http://educationendowmentfoundation.org.uk/news/teaching-assistants-can-improve-numeracy-and-literacy-when-used-effectively/

All schools should look at the Advisory, Conciliation and Arbitration Service (ACAS) Code of Practice, www.acas.org.uk

7. What Happens in the Classroom

Ensuring clarity of vision, ethos and strategic direction.
Holding the head teacher to account for the educational performance of the school and its pupils...

Everything that we have talked about so far has been at a distance from the pupils. The governors' role has been portrayed as dealing with data, meetings and reports. This much could apply to almost any kind of business. And while governors are expected to be businesslike in their way of working, there is the danger here of missing the point about schools. They are full of children.

Visiting the school

In 2011 Ofsted published a report on the features that it had identified as being characteristic of outstanding governing bodies (*School Governance: Learning from the best*). One of these was governors knowing their schools first hand. They spent time in their school during the working day, visited classrooms, walked the premises, and met the children and staff. They got to see children being taught and to talk to them.

Perhaps this is not so different from being the director of a commercial company. If the enterprise made car parts, you'd expect a director to want to see the factory floor when the parts were being manufactured, and if it was a chain of shops you'd expect him or her to visit some in opening times to see the merchandise on display and meet the staff and customers. To govern an institution you need to understand it, and to understand it you need to see it at work. It's only then that you will know what problems it has to deal with, how its staff work, and what effect the decisions that you have made are having on them and the business.

It can be difficult for busy school governors to find the time to visit their school during the day, especially if they have demanding jobs, but it's important to make the effort. It does not have to be done often. If you managed half a day twice a year it would be enough to give you some understanding, and you may well find that once you have gone in there's a desire to go again, which makes it easier to do. If you are new you should certainly ask to be shown round in school hours as part of your induction. And all schools have evening events, which, while not the same as teaching and learning in action, enrich your knowledge and usually provide a lot of entertainment at the same time.

Trustees of multi-academy trusts are unlikely to be able to visit all their schools, but each trustee can forge a link with a particular school and get to know it.

Visits by governors should have a purpose and a focus. Schools have different ways of organising them. One common method is for each governor to be linked to a subject or class, so that they talk to a single teacher to find out what the challenges and successes are in that class or subject, and can then receive reports on children's progress during the year. Some governors take on specific areas like special educational needs or ethnic minority children, which enables them to track how key statistical groups are doing. Some governing bodies arrange walks where a couple of governors will go round the school with the headteacher or other senior leader and visit several classrooms. Other governing bodies have whole days in their school, with a full governing body meeting, committees and plenty of time to visit classes, all on the same day.

The Ofsted report on outstanding governing bodies found examples of all of these, together with a common understanding of the need to identify the purpose of visits:

> Governors also visited their schools to talk to staff and pupils and to see the school in action. They used a range of formal and informal visits, including attending school events, conducting 'learning walks' and visiting classrooms. Crucially, effective practice involved a shared understanding of the purpose of the visit, how it was to be conducted and how it was to be reported back to the governing body and school leaders.

Many governing bodies have protocols on school visits, and there is guidance in various publications on how to develop a policy to make the visits effective. A common focus is to see how a policy is taking effect – say, the one on pupil behaviour – or to witness how interventions with struggling pupils are being managed. These involve talking to the principal in advance so that everyone is clear about what is to be achieved. The principal can then discuss the visit with the teachers affected, so that they too understand and can do any preparation.

Some teachers are quite sensitive about other adults coming to watch them at work. This is quite understandable as a lot of people would feel uneasy if a stranger or near-stranger came to look over their shoulder for a long time. They might think this is another form of observational assessment, such as is carried out by their line manager or Ofsted. It should be understood by all that the governor is not there to judge how well the teacher is doing their job. That is the role of the principal or the teacher's line manager, both of whom are professionals and know how to make that judgement. Even if the governor has teaching experience, perhaps as an ex-head, they should still not be making that kind of judgement. It is the school management's job, and we have seen how trying to do a manager's job for them undermines the principles on which governance is built. It would also, in this case, damage the confidence that teachers need to have in governors and would make it much harder for other governors to make successful visits. The prime aim of a governor's visit to school is not to judge but to learn.

Afterwards the governor should have a conversation with the principal or other school leader who arranged the visit to discuss what they have seen and ask any questions. This is the time to raise any matters that you thought were odd or possibly not good practice, and if something does need following up, the principal can do so. Most often it is a matter of something being explained that you might not have understood. Visits should also be reported back to the governing body, concentrating on the agreed focus of the visit, and thereby passing on useful information to the rest of the governors that everyone can benefit from. Often schools will have forms that have been specially designed for this. Pooling reports should help everyone govern the school better.

Ethos

What children learn at school is a preparation for the rest of their lives, so a school must give them the knowledge that they need in order to make informed decisions about their future. A secondary academy should try to work with local businesses and other employers to get their input into what is required of potential employees and to encourage them to come to the school to talk to and inspire pupils. Given that understanding the world of work must be an important part of a complete education, primary schools could do this too.

However, there is a wider aspect of the curriculum than just preparing pupils for going out to work. The *Governors' Handbook* gives two aims for the curriculum of maintained schools, which should apply also to academies:

- to promote the spiritual, moral, cultural, mental and physical development of pupils at the school and of society
- to prepare pupils at the school for the opportunities, responsibilities and experiences of later life.

The first point acts as a reminder that schools do not just give children knowledge and develop skills. They also inculcate moral standards, foster the potential to enjoy a full and rounded life, and help develop social skills. These points connect directly with a duty that all trusts hold, which is to determine, support and promote the ethos of the academy. If the school is a faith school its ethos is likely to be very apparent, but all schools will have an ethos of some kind. The following are extracts from ethos or vision statements from a variety of academies:

> "The pervading culture of the Academy will be one in which every student feels that they can succeed and in which their aspiration to be lifelong learners will be supported and encouraged. In addition we believe in and are committed to the development of the whole child, nurturing their personal and social skills, sense of enquiry, as well as their resilience to face life's challenges." (Ormiston Academy, Bushfield)

> "Reflect a culturally inclusive ethos.

> Emphasise the traditional values of self discipline, responsibility, respect, trust and cooperation." (Parkwood Academy, Sheffield)

> "We aim to develop inquiring, knowledgeable and caring young people who help to create a better, more peaceful and environmentally sustainable world through intercultural understanding and respect." (Parkside Federation Academies, Cambridge)

> "Whitley Academy is an innovative and inclusive school, committed to delivering high quality education for the community it serves. We value everyone that we work with, regardless of their differing needs, abilities and backgrounds. This ethos influences all that happens within the school – our mantra of 'deeds not words' supports all students to be the best they can be." (Whitley RSA Academy, Coventry)

It's easy enough to produce statements that sound aspirational and inclusive, but they are meaningless unless they are reflected in what and how the school teaches. Trustees and governors should hold the ethos in mind when asking about the teaching in the school. Is it really instilling a love of learning that will last through the children's lives, or has meeting targets become such a priority that children are being "crammed" without really developing an interest in their subjects? Is what is taught in English, history, art, RE and geography really "culturally diverse", or does it reinforce a traditional idea of what matters in Britain? Are children learning to respect the environment in a practical way, or only sitting in the classroom and learning about sustainability in science and geography? Is the school really producing creative young people if art, music and dance are given little support? Does valuing everyone in the school community mean not only respecting the cultures of ethnic minorities and working hard to raise the performance of children with special educational needs, but providing the means for the gifted and talented children to be stretched and develop their skills?

The curriculum

An area where the line between being strategic and being operational can seem hard to draw is the curriculum – what children learn.

As we have seen (in chapter 3) academies are not required to follow the National Curriculum. For some converter academies this was a large factor in their choosing to change status, for some others it scarcely counted and they have continued to teach it.

However, the curriculum extends beyond the subjects listed in the National Curriculum, or whatever an academy has put in place instead of it. It covers everything that is taught and learned in a school. Schools must at the very least also provide religious education and sex education, which are not included in the National Curriculum but the first of which is compulsory in both primary and secondary schools. The second is also compulsory in secondaries, while primary schools must decide whether to teach it. Primary school academies must also follow the Early Years Foundation Stage for children in Reception and, if they have them, in nursery classes, while secondaries must provide careers advice in Key Stage 4.

A broad and balanced curriculum

Deciding on the academy's curriculum is the responsibility for the trust/governing body. Some trusts have bought in professional advice from outside and drawn up the basics of the curriculum themselves. This is more likely to be the case where the trustees felt that the school was failing with the old curriculum and some radical change was needed, or where the trust has a strong ethos that called for major changes. Most trusts, on the other hand, would expect to be led by the principal and other senior members of staff. They are the ones that have to teach, with the professional knowledge of what can and cannot be achieved.

The governing body's responsibility is an overarching one, working, as you would expect, at the level of strategy. Its main job is to ensure that the school delivers "a broad and balanced curriculum". This has long been stipulated in law, and applies to all state schools. So although an academy may specialise in, say, science, the arts or business studies, it must still ensure that other subjects are fully and properly taught. It will have plenty of children who have no particular aptitude or interest in the specialism, and even those that do should leave the school with a rounded education. In fact, although academies are given a relatively free rein over their curricula, this is qualified by the condition that they must teach English, maths and science (except, in the case of the latter, alternative provision academies. i.e. PRUs that have converted).

Until recently maintained schools had to have a curriculum policy, and although this requirement has been removed it has been done in the spirit of reducing statutory requirements, not because governors are no longer expected to be interested in what is taught. That it was a requirement indicates the level at which governors should be involved. The policy would cover ensuring that the curriculum was broad and balanced, that assessment procedures were in place, that pupil attainment targets were set and that parents were informed of their children's progress. Governing bodies were not obliged to approve policies on individual subjects. Although the practice of these coming to the governing body was widespread, such policies address practical issues that should be left to the professionals.

Governors should ensure that parents know what curriculum is being on offer at the school, either through the website or in some other format.

Developing the curriculum

The curriculum is not fixed. A secondary school can at any time decide, for example, to change the modern languages on offer, promote individual sciences rather than single science or double science, start teaching dance or arrange the timetable so that no one can choose both geography and business studies. A primary school might introduce a range of languages into Key Stage 2, increase the amount of sport on offer and employ some part-time specialists, or develop a multi-cultural strand that runs through several subjects.

Such changes should come before the trust or, if the curriculum power is delegated, the local governing body. There are various questions you should ask when considering whether to agree changes:

- How will the pupils benefit from the change?

- How will the change impact on other areas of the curriculum?

- Will pupils perform as well, or better, in SATs tests or exams?

- How do the staff propose monitoring the impact of the proposed change on pupil performance?

- Do staff qualifications and training support the change? If additional training is required, is it available, how many members of staff will be involved and what will it cost?

- What new resources will be required to support the change? If any, are estimated costs available?

- Has an action plan been prepared for the introduction of change? What is the time scale and is it realistic?

(Carol Woodhouse, "Inputting into the Curriculum",
The School Governors' Yearbook 2006)

Religious education and collective worship

All state schools in England, at whatever phase, must teach religious education (RE). Unless the school has a faith designation, this should reflect the status of Christianity as the dominant faith in the British tradition. However, it should also take account of the other faiths that have substantial adherents here. Academies with a designated religion will provide religious education in accordance with the tenets of that religion. Religious education in these too is rarely entirely of one faith because the aim of RE should be to teach about religion in general, not to indoctrinate children into one particular one.

Academies are free to set their own curriculum for RE. In maintained schools determination of the religious syllabus is a local matter determined by the local Standing Advisory Council for Religious Education (SACRE). Academies may participate in the SACRE if all parties are in agreement, and those without a religious designation may follow the locally agreed syllabus if they so wish.

Non-faith schools sometimes neglect religious education. It is quite normal not to have specialist teachers in the subject, even at secondary level, so the teaching gets parcelled out. Ofsted looks at RE in the same way as it does other subjects and will penalise a school if it is taught poorly.

All schools and academies must also have a daily act of collective worship for their pupils. Unless the academy has a non-Christian religious designation this too must be of a broadly Christian nature. Parents can withdraw their children from RE and collective worship if they wish. Students over 16 can withdraw themselves from collective worship but not from RE; they have to be 18 to opt out of RE unilaterally.

Sex and relationships education

Secondary schools are required to deliver sex and relationships education, while primary schools are expected to deliver it. It can be a tricky subject as parental feelings can run high, especially among some of the ethnic minority groups in Britain. There is therefore some latitude about delivery: governors of primary schools can decide whether to teach it or not, and parents of pupils at any age have the right to withdraw them from sex education lessons. However, this does not extend to classes in other subjects, notably biology, that deal with the science of anatomy and reproduction.

The funding agreements of academies oblige them to have regard to guidance from the DfE on sex and relationships education. This specifies that the governing body should draw up a policy in consultation with the parents which reflects the wishes of parents and the local community.

The policy should place sex education in the context of developing loving and stable relationships. It should not just impart knowledge, including knowledge about safe sex, but should also address attitudes and values and aim to develop social and personal skills. According to the DfE guidance current at the time of writing, "The policy must:

- define sex and relationship education;

- describe how sex and relationship education is provided and who is responsible for providing it

- say how sex and relationship education is monitored and evaluated

- include information about parents' right to withdrawal

- be reviewed regularly."

Sex and Relationship Education Guidance (DfEE, 2000)

Preparing children for life in modern Britain

One outcome of the "Trojan Horse" affair, where a group of governors were suspected to be using their influence to encourage schools to promote radical Islamicist beliefs, is that all schools are now expected to have greater regard for the teaching of spiritual, moral, social and cultural (SMSC) values. This includes promoting what are loosely called "British values". The government defines these in guidance as "democracy, the rule of law, individual liberty, and mutual respect and tolerance of those with different faiths and beliefs".

Schools are expected not just to instil these through the curriculum but in other ways, such as encouraging democratic processes through the school council, using extra-curricular activities to promote democratic values, and organising visits to local councils, parliament and places of worship of different religious faiths. Governors should ensure that the school is providing good quality SMSC in the curriculum and its other activities, and that it is having a positive impact on pupils' understanding and awareness.

Ofsted now looks at how successfully schools teach SMSC and British values, and factors this in their judgement of the school.

Behaviour

A considerable emphasis has been given in recent years to pupil behaviour in schools, to the extent that it is one of the four areas of Ofsted inspection.

Behaviour is important not only its own right. Disruptive behaviour means that the perpetrator is not concentrating on learning, and is making it harder for other children to learn. But poor behaviour may distract no one other than the child concerned; you may hear the term "behaviour for learning" used by teachers, which refers to whether children engage with learning. They may instead idle away their time day-dreaming or doodling. Good behaviour is also a skill for life; not many employers relish taking on staff who are going to spend their time throwing screwed up balls of paper or distracting other people with silly remarks.

An academy trust is required to ensure that there is a full behaviour policy drawn up by the principal, setting out the expectations of behaviour and what will be done about poor behaviour. In practice it is likely to be a lengthy document that incorporates practice as well as policies, spelling out what sanctions will be applied to poor behaviour and when.

Not only should the policy exist but it should be known by all the staff, while the principles behind it should be explained to the parents. "All the staff" means teaching assistants and the rest of the support staff as pupils will regularly interact with office staff, caretakers and midday supervisors, and are as likely to misbehave in front of them as much as they are in class – perhaps more so. Behaviour problems often arise in schools because staff do not have a consistent approach. Children will simply be confused if they find something that they do in front of one staff member passes without comment from them but earns a reprimand if repeated in front of another, while some other children will exploit any differences of approach to their own advantage.

Governors are not obliged to approve the policy but should discuss the principles behind it, rather than the detail. The latter should come first, and it will establish the groundwork on which the detailed policy will be built. Finding the desired point in the ranges from of tolerance to strictness and from self-discipline to authority will be guided by the school's agreed ethos.

The effectiveness of the policy is easily observed on a school visit. Whereas a governor should not judge the quality of teaching, we can be more confident when it comes to noticing how pupils behave. Governors should not try to punish any poor behaviour or put it down as a black mark against the teacher but you can react as you would with anyone else's child, providing you do it in the context of the behaviour policy that you have agreed. Any such instances are also something to discuss afterwards. Staff well know who the troublemakers are in their school and will often have worked out ways of dealing with them which may not be apparent in a short visit. When it comes to general class behaviour older governors may be surprised by what is acceptable today. Children are no longer expected to work in attentive silence throughout a class, but there are times when a bit of hubbub is a sign that they are fully engaged, especially during group activities.

SEN and disabilities

All state schools have duty to teach children with Special Educational Needs (SEN). In so doing they must have regard to *The Special Educational Needs Code of Practice*, and governors must agree a policy on SEN that follows what it says. It should give basic information on the school's provision for SEN, how it identifies and provides for pupils with SEN, its staffing policies for teaching these pupils and how it works with other schools. Although oversight of provision for pupils with SEN can be delegated to a committee, the SEN policy has to be agreed at a full meeting of the trust/governing body.

All schools have to employ a Special Educational Needs Coordinator (SENCO), who is responsible for implementation of the policy across the school, and must have received special training in the role.

Governors also have a specific duty to publish information on the school website about the implementation of the governing body's policy on pupils with special educational needs and any changes to the policy during the last year. It is normal for the principal or SENCO to write this statement, but governors must make sure it is done and posted every year. They should also treat it like any report on provision for a group of children in the school, which is to understand it and use it as a basis for challenge, if necessary.

The system of classifying and meeting special educational years that had been in place for many years was overhauled in a long process starting in 2010 and culminating in September 2014. Under the old system special educational needs were categorised according to three levels of severity: school action (the least severe), school action plus, and statements of special educational needs (the most severe). The new system abolishes school action and school action plus because it was thought that these gave an unnecessary label to pupil ability or behaviour that were not abnormal and which could be addressed by standard intervention measures. Children thought possibly to need special support will be assessed, and if it is found necessary will be given an education and health care (EHC) plan. Those given statements of special educational needs under the old system are to have them replaced by EHC plans before April 2018.

The EHC plan should specify the short- and long-term outcomes expected for the child and the means to be provided to achieve them. The plan is also intended, as is apparent from the name, to involve other agencies that supply support to the child, not just schools. The responsibility for bringing together the various agencies rests with the local authority, even if the child is currently attending an academy. The parents and children should also take part in drawing up the plan and can specify a school they want the child to attend. Academies, like maintained schools, are required to cooperate with the local authority and must admit the child if identified in the plan, unless they can show that to do so would harm the education of other children and that there are no reasonable steps they can take to avoid this.

SEN is often combined with supporting children with disabilities, and the acronym SEND is commonly used (Special Educational Needs and Disabilities). The definition in the Equality Act 2010 encourages this combination by saying that you are disabled if you have "a physical or mental impairment that has a 'substantial' and 'long-term' negative effect on your ability to do normal daily activities". Despite the fact that there is an overlap, disabled children may not have SEN: they can find it have difficult to get around the school, but have no problems with learning once they are in the classroom. Or their disabilities may prevent their doing things that are a normal part of learning, such as using a pen, in which case they have a direct affect on their level of attainment. Children may have special educational needs that have nothing to do with a physical or mental impairment, such as if their reading levels are very poor because they suffer from neglect.

Schools, including academies, are required to do what they can to help disabled children, such as buying special equipment for them. Often there are grants for this. The obligation includes making the premises as accessible as possible. According to the 2010 Equality Act all schools must have a written plan which aims to:

- increase the extent to which pupils can participate in the school's curriculum

- improve the physical environment of the school for the purpose of increasing the extent to which disabled pupils are able to take advantage of education and benefits, facilities or services provided or offered by the school

- improve the delivery to disabled pupils of information which is readily accessible to pupils who are not disabled.

However, a principle of reasonableness applies. The action required should be consonant with the provision of education to other children and the efficient use of resources. A tall Victorian school, for example, would not be expected to put in a lift at vast expense to accommodate a pupil in a wheelchair. But if the school were building a new multi-storey block, then a lift should be included in the plans.

The accessibility plan must be reviewed every three years, though progress on implementation should be examined at least yearly.

Statutory guidance for schools and others in supporting children and young people with special educational needs and disabilities is published by the DfE in the SEND Code of Practice. Governors with special responsibilities for SEN should also familiarise themselves with the document. It is available on Gov.uk.

Further information

School visits
David Marriott, *Monitoring and Evaluation: A practical guide for school governors*, Adamson Publishing, 3rd edition 2011

Curriculum
Guidance is on Gov.uk; search "Curriculum"

British Values
DfE, *Promoting Fundamental British Values as Part of SMSC in Schools: Departmental advice for maintained schools*, www.gov.uk

DfE, *Improving the Spiritual, Moral, Social and Cultural (SMSC) Development of Pupils: Departmental advice and supplementary guidance for independent schools, academies and free schools*, www.gov.uk

Pupil Behaviour
DfE, *Behaviour and Discipline in Schools: Guidance for governing bodies*, www.gov.uk

Special Educational Needs and Disabilities
See Gov.uk for the SEND Code of Practice and other guidance documents.

Disability Discrimination Act Code of Practice for Schools, www.equalityhumanrights.com/advice-and-guidance/information-for-advisers/codes-of-practice

The NCTL website has a range of guidance documents for governors on www.gov.uk

8. Statutory Responsibilities

Academies and free schools have greater freedoms than maintained schools in relation to school policies and other documents. Where relevant, arrangements applying to these schools are outlined in legislation or in their funding agreements, which may vary between individual academies and free schools.

DfE, *Policies and Other Documents That Governing Bodies and Proprietors are Required to Have by Law*

Admissions

Unlike most (but not all) maintained schools, academies are their own admissions authorities; in other words, they determine their admissions criteria. For the majority of maintained schools the admission authority is the local authority.

There are two essential documents for anyone involved in admissions: the *School Admissions Code* and the *Admission Appeals Code* (both frequently revised; see Gov.uk for the latest versions). These Codes give statutory guidance, which means that all admission authorities, including academies, must comply with them. They also highlight the distinction between what must be done and what should be done.

Despite the impression often given by the Press and politicians, parents do not have an absolute right to choose a school for their child, but can only state a preference. If a school is not full, it must accept any applicant who wants a place (except for selective schools, including grammar schools that have become academies). This includes faith schools that do not have enough applicants of their own faith to fill the places available for them.

A school is deemed to be full when it has reached its published admission number (PAN) for the age group when children are normally admitted. Applicants who have expressed a preference for the school but are not offered a place have a right to appeal to an independent appeal panel, and the school must inform them of this.

All schools, including academies, have to publish their admission arrangements, which they must draw up by the end of February each year for the September of the following year. Even academies have to submit their admissions arrangements to the local authority, but this is for information not approval, as LAs have the job of coordinating admissions across their area. If there are more applicants than places, allocations are made according to the published policy, which includes over-subscription criteria, in order of importance. The Admissions Code prohibits unfair over-subscription criteria, and states that priority must be given to looked-after children. It explains what criteria are acceptable, which often include:

- a brother or sister at the school

- a medical or social need for that school

- nearness to the school and how distance or catchment area is determined

- feeder schools

- in church schools, church membership

- aptitude, in those specialist schools which select some places by this criterion, but they must state how this will be assessed.

Admissions authorities decide on the priority order of these and any other criteria they use. No admission authority (except for boarding schools) may use interviewing parents or children as part of the admissions process. They should also avoid having school rules or requirements that may deter less well-off parents from applying, such as specifying a school uniform that is expensive to buy.

Excluding pupils from the school

The decision to exclude a pupil is a headteacher's/principal's, but governing bodies are required to consider all permanent and various fixed-term pupil exclusions and may overturn them. This power is commonly delegated by trusts to local governing bodies.

Exclusions are not considered by the whole governing body but by a specially constituted panel. This can be a standing discipline committee that is appointed annually to be on hand at any time that an exclusion arises, or it may be drawn from a pool of governors who volunteer to serve as and when hearings are needed. The minimum number allowed on a panel is three.

The panel's duty is to review all permanent exclusions, all fixed-term exclusions that bring the total number of days that the pupil has been excluded during the term to over 15, and all fixed-term exclusions that will result in the pupil missing a public exam. This includes half-day or lunchtime exclusions. Parents may appeal against any exclusion, including those of 15 days or less. If the exclusion does not bring the pupil's total to over five days in one term the panel has to consider the parent's points (which must be put in writing), and can agree to meet the parent, though it does not have to. If the pupil's exclusions total more than five days in one term the panel must not only consider the parent's written points but must also invite the parent to the review meeting.

The hearings must be clerked, and someone else must be employed to do this if the governing body clerk is not able to.

The panel can only uphold the exclusion or direct the pupil's reinstatement; it cannot increase the length of an exclusion should it feel that the principal has been too lenient. The standard of proof required in assessing whether the pupil did whatever it is that caused the exclusion should be based "on the balance of probabilities", not on certainty. This has been clarified by government guidance: "it is more probable than not that the pupil did what s/he is alleged to have done". There is a caveat that the more serious the allegation, the more convincing the evidence needs to be.

When a panel decides to uphold the exclusion, the pupil's parents may appeal to a review panel if they consider that the school acted improperly in enforcing the exclusion. The review panel has then to be set up by the academy but is independent of it. It does not have the power to overthrow an exclusion decision, but may direct the governing body to reconsider it if it thinks that the process was flawed.

There is a strong expectation that governors who sit on discipline committees and all those who sit on independent exclusion appeal panels should have received appropriate training.

Removing pupils from school other than by exclusion

There are two circumstances in which a pupil may be removed from the school other than by formal exclusion. Both are exceptional:

- where a pupil has been accused of a serious criminal offence outside the school's jurisdiction and there is insufficient evidence to warrant exclusion but there are compelling reasons why the pupil should not be in the school

- where the pupil's presence would be a serious health and safety risk to others in the school. The removal may only be carried out for medical reasons and after consultation with the parents.

"Informal exclusions", where the head and parent agree that it would be best if the pupil was removed from school without being registered as excluded, are expressly forbidden by regulations.

Handling complaints

All schools and academies have to have complaints procedures.

Complaints may come from any of a variety of sources. Most complainants are parents, but a complaint may come from a pupil, a member of staff or a member of the general public.

There are various principles that the complaints procedure should follow:

- It needs to be simple, quick and confidential, with a clear timetable.

- It should encourage resolution by informal methods wherever possible.

- It should be fair and impartial, and be perceived to be so.

- It should be effective in resolving complaints and in providing appropriate redress where necessary.

- It should be publicised – such as on the school website or in a separate document to be given to new parents and others. If appropriate it should be published in community languages.

- It should provide information to senior management so that faults or deficiencies can be rectified.

The statutory requirements for dealing with complaints from parents are set out in the *Education (Independent School Standards) (England) Regulations 2010*. They say that the procedure must contain at least three stages, though some schools have four. The first is an informal stage where the complaint is taken up with a senior member of staff, possibly the principal. This stage is sometimes split in two, with the complaint first going to the member of staff involved, and only then being referred upwards if it cannot be settled there. If the complaint cannot be resolved at either of these, then the complainant formally puts their case in writing to the chair of governors. If it is still not resolved, the complainant can then ask for a formal hearing, where they can state why they were not satisfied with the responses given by the school.

As with exclusions, the hearing is before a panel set up by the trust and consisting of at least three people, who must not be "tainted" by prior knowledge of the details of the complaint or with any involvement in the matters complained about. One of these people must be totally independent of the school. Both the complainant and the principal put their case in person to the panel. The panel deliberates in private and makes its ruling. Its decision is final, except that the complainant can appeal to the Education Funding Agency if they feel that the governing body has not followed its own complaints procedure or its duties as set out in its funding agreement, or failed to meet its legal obligations. The EFA cannot overturn the academy's decision, but can direct it to reconsider.

Academies can choose how they handle complaints received from people who are not parents of pupils in the school: whether to follow the same procedure as for parents or to have a different one.

Care needs to be taken with complaints about the actions of specific members of staff. These should generally be dealt with under the school's disciplinary procedure, under which the staff member will have the right to be heard and to be represented by their union. If a parent is not satisfied with this, then their complaint should be handled as a complaint against the way the school handled the matter, rather than against the individual.

Food standards

Standards stating the types of food and drink that should be provided in pupil lunches apply to maintained schools and to some academies. Academies established after 2010 were not obliged to follow the food standards in place at the time, and new standards that came into force in January 2015 are also currently not mandatory for them. However, academies created after 1 September 2014 have a requirement to follow the standards written into their funding agreements.

Legally required documents

Policies

Governing bodies have to agree a number of policies designed to ensure that the school complies with the law, is well managed and provides a safe environment for those that study and work in it. The list of such policies varies from time to time according to changes in legislation and interpretation of legislation, so the DfE's publication *Statutory Policies for Schools* should be consulted regularly (on Gov.uk). The clerk should be asked to keep a list of the governing body's policies, with a note of who approves them (trust, local governing body, committee) and the date when they have to be reviewed. The policies should also be available for staff and parents to see; usually they are posted on the school's website.

The statutory policies are not the same for academies and maintained schools, and *Statutory Policies for Schools* states for each policy what type of school it applies to. The following lists those for academies at the time of writing, with notes to explain what they are.

Charging and remissions

Schools must determine the criteria according to which they will charge the parents of pupils for activities and who qualifies for financial support. Schools are not allowed to charge for activities that take place during the formal school day, other than at lunchtime or for musical tuition that is not part of the core curriculum.

Child protection policy and procedures

All staff should know the procedure for dealing with children who it is suspected are being abused, should equip children with the skills to keep themselves safe, including on the Internet, and ensure that the school is a safe place for them. This includes having safeguarding procedures in place when recruiting staff (see Staffing chapter).

Data protection

A school is obliged under the Data Protection Act 1998 to ensure that it only keeps information about pupils and staff that it needs, that the information is secure, relevant and up to date, and that there is a procedure for individuals to see information held about them.

Health and safety

The trust is responsible for the health and safety of all people on the premises, including staff, pupils and visitors, and for school members when taking part in school activities off site. It must take reasonable steps to ensure that the buildings and contents are safe and that risk assessments are made, and must ensure that the school maintains records of their state and of any incidents that occur.

Pupil behaviour

See chapter 7.

Sex and relationships education

See chapter 7.

Special educational needs and disabilities

See chapter 7.

Other statutory documents

There are various other documents that a governing body should ensure that an academy has compiled and complies with.

Admissions arrangements statement

See above.

Accessibility Plan

See chapter 7.

Allegations of Abuse against Staff, Procedure for Handling

See chapter 6.

Complaints procedure

See above.

Central record of recruitment checks

Details of the checks made on new members of staff, including checking their Disclosure and Barring Service (DBS) certificates, must be kept together in one place, be up to date and be available for inspection. It is normal practice for one governor to undertake responsibility for ensuring periodically that this has been done.

Early Years Foundation Stage

Governors of all schools that cater for children at any stage from birth to the end of the academic year in which they have their fifth birthday are required to ensure that their schools deliver the Early Years Foundation Stage.

Freedom of information scheme

State schools are public organisations and therefore, under the Freedom of Information Act 2000, must have a scheme in place for responding to requests for disclosure of information. It will specify the procedure for providing the information, together with a timetable, what information will not be provided (according to the legal parameters) and the circumstances in which a charge will be made.

Premises management

This relates to health and safety. There are many aspects of a public building that require safe management, and where those requirements are spelled out in regulations. Governing bodies should ensure that staff responsible for buildings are aware of the appropriate compliance and guidance documents and comply with what they say.

Register of pupils' admissions to school

Governors should ensure that the school maintains a complete and up-to-date register.

Register of pupils' attendance

Governors should ensure that the school keeps daily registers of present and absent pupils.

Procedures for addressing staff discipline, conduct and grievance

See chapter 6.

Whistleblowing procedures

Academy trusts must make sure that suitable procedures are in place for staff who wish to raise concerns about financial or other management.

There are also statutory requirements about financial reporting which we have looked at in chapter 5, on finance.

What governing bodies have to publish

The corollary of greater autonomy is greater accountability. If schools are given a relatively free hand in how they spend public money, the public has the right to know a lot about what they are doing with it.

Extensive accountability involves transparency. Public attention focuses on the key performance indicators. Accordingly, all state schools have to publish information on key indicators of what they are doing for their children's education. While School Performance Tables are published in the Press showing how schools rate in comparison with each other on their headline SATs or GCSE results, schools also have to publish this information themselves on their websites and provide a link to the DfE tables. In addition they must post up the latest Ofsted report on the school or provide a link to it.

Primary schools must publish information on how much Pupil Premium they receive, how they have used it and what effect it is having (see chapter 4). Secondary schools must publish how much Year 7 Literacy and Numeracy Catch-up Premium they received and how it was spent. Primary schools also receive a special PE and Sport Grant (see chapter 4). A primary school's website must state how much they receive, what it has been spent on and what impact it has had.

All schools must publish details of their policy on provision for pupils with special educational needs or disabilities. They must also publish the equality objective they draw up every four years and each year a statement about how they are meeting their public duty on equality.

In addition, basic information about an academy must be available on the website or otherwise made available to parents:

- the address, phone number and name of the principal

- the curriculum, by academic year and subject

- the school's ethos

- the opening times of the school

- the charging and remissions policy

- the school's policies on and arrangements for admissions, pupil discipline and exclusions

- the arrangements for combating bullying and for securing health and safety

- the complaints procedure and number of complaints received during the previous year

- information about the annual report and financial statements

- information about the trust's memorandum, articles of association and funding agreement

- the names of trustees and members and the register of their interests, including any close family relationships between members and trustees, or members or trustees and employees

- the structure and remit of the members, trust, committees and local governing bodies, and the names of the chairs of each

- the attendance record of trustees and local governors.

Other information may be specified in the funding agreement.

Schools must also send parents an annual written report of their child's progress and attainment in the main subject areas taught.

Further information

School Admissions Code on Gov.uk under Publications

Complaints Procedure Toolkit, on Gov.uk

EFA, *Setting up an Academies Complaints Procedure*, on Gov.uk

9. Relationships

The determining relationship for any academy local governing body in a chain is with its trust. The trust provides direction for the governing body and practical support for the school. Those on local governing bodies cannot function properly without knowing the terms of the relationship in their own chain. The situation, however, is different for Church schools, which are special cases and which are discussed shortly.

Internal relationships

Chair and principal

"The relationship between them [the headteacher and the chair] is the most important aspect of the chair's role"

> Headteacher quoted in *The Chair of the School Governing Body in England: Roles, relationships and responsibilities* (CfBT, 2013)

The corporate nature of a governing body means that the chair has very few executive powers beyond that of any other governor, other than for tasks that have been specifically delegated to him or her. Nevertheless, the chair is in a privileged position and will receive a lot of information before it gets to other governors. There will also be a lot more information that is not appropriate to pass on.

The source of this is the chair's close relationship with the principal. We have talked in this book so far about the need for the governing body to challenge the principal. This remains true, but there is more to how the chair works with the principal. The chair has a role of both confidante and brother-in-arms with the principal. How well this sometimes tricky relationship works is critical to the successful governance of the school.

Research was conducted into the chair's role by academics from the universities of Bath, Warwick and Glamorgan and the Institute of Education in 2012 and 2013. The resulting document, *The Chair of the School Governing Body in England: Roles, relationships and responsibilities* (CfBT, 2013), described how various pairs of heads and chairs managed their roles. One chair summed up for all in saying: "I can't imagine what it would be like if this was not an open and honest relationship."

Success is not a matter of the two becoming best mates any more than it is of one of two boxers circling each other looking to inflict a blow. It comes through building trust and respect, and learning to work closely but maintaining some distance. Chairs who become too friendly with their heads/principals can lose the perspective that enables them to cast a critical eye on what the leadership of the school is doing. Equally, those who see their job as being to criticise everything that the principal does will soon antagonise him or her, who will then become defensive, selective in what they share and less likely to see what is constructive in the stream of scepticism. One of the commonly used descriptions of successful relationships that the researchers found was "professional"; others that came up included "honest", "respectful" and "open".

The chair of the governing body needs to learn how to hold this privileged position while respecting the corporate responsibility of the governing body. There are no text book rules here, as this is a balance that each person has to learn to strike for themselves. The nature of the confidences you receive will depend on the strength of the relationship, as well as the personalities of the two parties. Any principal should feel that they can discuss instances of pupil misbehaviour or distress, and they should also be able to have a frank conversation about staffing issues. Being a principal can be a lonely job, and often the chair is the only person in the school with whom they can chew over their problems. These may, if the relationship is strong, include those of a personal nature, whether letting off steam or sharing an emotional crisis. Given the importance of succession planning, chairs should also feel that they can ask principals if they are thinking of moving on or retiring, and principals should be able to answer secure in the knowledge that what they say will not go any further.

The chair, therefore, may receive some information that cannot be shared with the rest of the governing body. But there are things that a chair should explain must be shared, especially those that are not just for information but which require a decision. For example, the chair and principal are more than likely to discuss altering the curriculum from time to time, and they could come to the point where they both agreed that a change was necessary, but this would have to go the governors for discussion and approval. Other matters will require some sort of action to be taken whose ultimate purpose is not immediately explicit. For example, if the principal did inform the chair in confidence that he or she were going to retire at the end of the school year, the chair might decide that this was a good time for the governing body to think about its aims for the school, and where it wanted it to go over the next few years.

However, a working relationship that is effective in sharing and passing on information can risk making the principal and chair seem to others like a double act. They may appear to be constantly asking the governing body to do no more than endorse decisions that they have jointly already made. This can be avoided if the chair and principal do not always seek first to resolve differences of opinion in private, but instead they agree to be frank about their views at the governing body and leave the decision to arise from open discussion. The balance to be struck here is between appearing on the one hand to stitch everything up in advance and on the other being so far apart that the school lacks clear direction.

Detailed guidance is available on making this relationship work, both in published form and in training courses, while new chairs will find it covered in the Chairs of Governors' Leadership Development Programme produced by the National College for Teaching and Leadership and offered throughout the country. The National Governors' Association (NGA) has produced a two-page document jointly with the two headteacher associations, the National Association of Headteachers (NAHT) and the Association of School and College Leaders (ASCL), together with the Local Government Association (LGA) that defines what governing bodies and headteachers should expect of each other. Being endorsed by both heads and governors, *What Governing Boards Should Expect from School Leaders and What School Leaders Should Expect from Governing Boards* has the strength that any chair or head in dispute over mutual expectations can quote a document approved by the national representative body of the other.

There are two points to add that are specific to academies.

Chairs of single academy trusts have a more wide-ranging role than chairs of maintained school governing bodies. The chair of the governing body is automatically also a member of the trust board (unless the trust has gained an exemption from the DfE's model Articles of Association). They may even be the chair of the trust. They are therefore indisputably the employer of the principal and the other staff. This can affect the balance of the relationship with the principal, who knows that they are dealing with their boss when talking to the chair.

The same may apply in a multi-academy trust, if the chair of the local governing body is also a member of the trust board. However, there is no requirement for them to be. If they are not, then the chair really needs to know thoroughly what powers have been delegated to the local governing body, and which ones remain with the trust. They also have to bear in mind that the principal will have a separate relationship with the trust, and will be receiving strategic direction from it. The chair should be fully aware of what this is; if they are not, then the local governing body cannot do its work.

However, if the headteacher disagrees seriously with the local governing body chair, they may turn to the trust for support, and if obtained it can undermine the chair's authority.

Parents

"Parental engagement can be a powerful lever for raising achievement in schools and there is much research to show the value of schools and parents working together to support pupils' learning."

Ofsted, *Schools and Parents*, 2011

The parental voice has always been considered sufficiently important for it to be compulsory to have parent governors in all state schools, even though for both academies and for maintained schools in recent years there are few other prescriptions about who should sit on a governing body.

According to the DfE's model Articles of Association, each academy must have at least two parent governors elected by the parents. In a single academy trust this guarantees their representation on the trust. For multi-academy trusts the model Articles specify that there must be at least two parent directors on the trust board, unless there are local governing bodies that include two parents. This will generally be the case, because the model funding agreement for academies specifies that each academy in a trust will have its own local governing body (called an "advisory body" in the model) which will have a minimum of two elected parent governors. Older academies, set up before the Academies Act 2010, have a minimum of only one parent governor. How the election is conducted across several schools is left up to the trustees, with the proviso that voting must be by secret ballot.

Like other trustees, parents elected to the board are elected for four years, irrespective of whether their child leaves the school during this time. They can resign before the completion of this term, if they so wish. The term of office for governors serving on local governing bodies is determined by the trust.

Parent governors are not delegates but representatives. Nevertheless, parent governors should endeavour to ascertain parents' views on significant matters so that they can report them to the governing body, even if they do not agree with them. This is one of the most important functions of parent governors that marks them out as different from the rest. How they ascertain these views will often just be through conversations in the playground, but there are formal methods such as through attending the parent council (if the school has one) or PTA. Really important matters, such as changing the school uniform, call for formal consultation.

Parent governors can find themselves under more pressure than other governors, not only to support positions taken by other parents but to report to them on what happened at governing body meetings. It's fine to do this objectively by telling people of decisions that were made (unless the matter was deemed confidential), but parent governors in particular need to be aware of corporate responsibility and confidentiality. You should not divulge who said what at a governing body meeting, and it is also completely inappropriate to say in public that you did not support a majority view. Where there are breaches of confidentiality in a governing body, often the offenders are parents. Many governing bodies have a code of practice or of conduct that makes clear what the rules are.

Having parent governors is not the end of a school's responsibilities to parents; it is just the beginning. The previous chapter listed all the items that a school must publish. These are public documents, but the main beneficiaries are expected to be to parents, who can then look at the school's curriculum, its results, and its policies, etc. The chapter also noted that the school must send each parent a report once a year on their child's progress. This will be the most important element of reporting for most parents, as even the most altruistic parent is going to be primarily concerned with their own child. Most schools do much more, holding parents' evenings where parents can discuss their children's progress with teachers and a host of events that parents are invited to attend.

There have been various studies that show that parental involvement is a huge factor in a child's performance at school. Even though social background is also a great determinant of eventual outcomes, a child is more likely to succeed at school if he or she comes from a poor background but has parents who are passionately involved in helping with their education than if they come from a rich background where they are neglected. It might seem difficult for a parent of a truculent teenager to believe that their influence counts for much, but it certainly does when children are younger. After all, a child only spends about 23% of its waking hours at school, averaged out over the school year.

Governors need to ensure that the school welcomes parents and does what it can to engage them in its work. These days the former is normal, but engaging some parents remains a challenge. However, there are decisions that governors can make that help, such as employing a Parent Support Adviser, whose role is to contact parents who are struggling with difficult children or whom the school rarely or never sees.

Working outside the school

The community

"The academy will be at the heart of its community, promoting community cohesion and sharing facilities with other schools and the wider community"

DfE, *Model Funding Agreement for Academies and Free Schools*,
December 2013

Academies were set up to enjoy and exploit autonomy. But at the same time, as the above quote makes abundantly clear, they are expected both to work with other schools and to embrace their local communities.

A paradox or a corrective? Certainly, academies are autonomous, but they are there to serve the children in the locality, and they can only do this fully by remaining a major player in that community. They are meant to experiment and develop creative solutions, but not just for their own benefit. They are meant to feed into the educational system by supporting other schools, with whom they should share any good practice they have developed. While they are independent schools, they are still state schools.

For governors, sharing facilities is easy to grasp, as it requires no more than ensuring that academies do what maintained schools already do: open up their premises for use by community groups, and encourage those groups to take up the offer. Although it is not compulsory, it is sensible for governing bodies to ensure that the school has a lettings policy that they have discussed and agreed.

There is more to working with the community than just ensuring that the school hall can be made available to a Pilates class. Many governors in academies hold significant positions within the local society, either through their work, faith group or voluntary activity. Governors are therefore well placed to identify opportunities for developing contacts that will further children's education. This can be by arranging visits by employers, advising the school in advance of opportunities to engage with the arts, identifying voluntary activities in which children can participate so as to develop their sense of social responsibility, or introducing customs and celebrations from the variety of ethnic groups in the area. While it is not a governing body decision whether to follow up on any of these, governors can enrich a school by sharing their contacts and knowledge of the outside world.

A school has an important place in any community. Many adults who live nearby will have attended it. Many others will have children of their own or children of other family members in it. It is likely to be a prominent building that stands out. Children will be very visible as they enter and leave. In rural communities it may be the only facility that is left after others have been closed. People who have no other connection with it will be used to going into the premises for sporting, cultural or social activities.

Schools therefore have an important role in promoting cohesion between the different ethnic, religious and social groups that make up the community in which they are located. A few years ago Ofsted used to look at how well schools promoted this duty. They no longer do this – although it is something they will be aware of in making their judgements – but the questions they used are good ones for governors to ask of their schools:

> How does school provide for specific groups within its teaching and curriculum?

> Given this, how successful is school in evaluating its effectiveness through increased contact with the parents and carers of these groups?

> Are these groups represented on the governing body, and if not how does school seek and use their views?

The last question is particularly pertinent in light of the "Trojan Horse" case in Birmingham. Among its other lessons, this highlighted that engagement with different community groups does not have to be through representation on the governing body, but can, and should, be done through other means as well.

Other schools
"If you're converting as a stand-alone school you will be expected to support another local school when you become an academy."

DfE website

A community need not just be the immediate area around a school. Community is like an onion, a collection of layers around a common centre. We have the community of our street, that of our part of town, the whole town, our region, the country. We also have other, non geographical communities: our friends, who may be scattered around the world; fellow supporters of our football team; people in our line of work; people who share our enthusiasm for particular hobbies; and so on. For many academies, there is an easily identified community, that of other academies in the trust, irrespective of geography.

Politicians of all colours recognise the value of schools working together. Academy chains are not the only way of doing this, but they are a powerful one. All academies are expected to work with other schools, as the above quote from the DfE makes clear.

Many local authorities encourage academies to remain part of the "local family of schools", and often they are only too happy to do so. For one thing, academies can access support, guidance and training from local authority governor services, if appropriate. There is an imperative, anyway, for secondary academies to continue to work with their feeder schools. A school does not cease to be part of a cluster because it has become an academy; it's just that the sharing of any funds becomes a bit more complex.

For parents and some governors there can be a resistance to working with others. It's sometimes argued that lending a principal or a high-quality teacher to another school for a part of the week over a long period or for a whole term is a hazard for the lender. It should be a governing body decision whether to do this, and governors are right to ask challenging questions about the possible effect on the school and to seek reassurance that quality will not decline. However, it should also be borne in mind that all the evidence suggests that good schools have no problem with this as there is plenty of support to fill the gaps. When it comes to lending a principal, this provides an opportunity for a deputy to step up, enabling them to improve their own practice and also to introduce a new perspective. The principal is likely to benefit from the experience too. Teaching is a profession that needs constant renewal; a good teacher is a good learner and is always looking out for opportunities to develop professionally. Teachers can easily get stuck in their classrooms, and it's an unusual teacher who does not recognise that they will improve from going out and watching how others perform. So when the person lent is a classroom teacher, they usually come back professionally enriched and their teaching practice refined.

Faith schools

In addition to the task of governing the school in accordance with the Education Acts and ensuring that it provides the best possible education for all its pupils, the governors of a faith school ... have the duty of maintaining the school's special character."
Joan Sallis, *Foundation Governors:Your own guide*, 2006

Voluntary schools that convert to academy status are specially provided for in legislation. The government intends that there should be no change in their faith affiliation or in the governance arrangements, and accordingly has produced different model Articles of Association for church schools. There are no such models for academies of other faiths, but they may use them as models in negotiating Articles that are right for them.

There are different sets of these models for new Church academies. They have been agreed with the Church of England and the Catholic Church. One model replicates that of Anglican voluntary aided schools, where the trust appoints the majority of the governors; another replicates that of a voluntary controlled school, where it appoints some but only a minority of the governors; while a separate model is primarily for Catholic schools, though it may also be used by Church of England schools if the school and diocese agree that it is the most appropriate one. Any change in the Articles needs to be agreed by the bishop and the trustees.

There is normally more prescription about the membership of a governing body of a faith academy than there is of other academies. The rules are quite complicated, and will be given in the Articles of Association, but basically there must be two elected parent governors, there may be two staff governors and the governing body may co-opt up to two members. The faith has the right to specify a number of other governors, including *ex officio* governors such as the incumbent, the dean and the bishop. However, under the second model (as with voluntary controlled schools) these governors and any others appointed to represent the faith – the "Foundation" governors – cannot make up more than 25 percent of the governing body. Under the other models the governors representing the faith form the majority.

It's obvious from this that governing bodies in faith academies are expected to have a close link with the Church (or other faith). Those governors who do not actually represent it are required to support its ethos.

Could it be difficult to maintain that link with the faith, in the same way as it can be hard for schools to engage with their communities? Actually, it is unlikely that that would be the case, as people who work for the faith are represented on the governing body and many of the other governors are regular worshippers. Moreover, for church academies, most dioceses are keen to support their schools. They will take an active role in doing this, receiving and if necessary responding to governing body minutes, and will often provide practical help with training and helping in making senior appointments.

The governors are expected to ensure that the academy acts in accordance with its ethos. Governors should hold it in mind and be guided by it when making decisions, especially those that have a moral dimension. Even parents who expressed a preference for the school without actively sharing its faith will often have chosen it because they value its caring, ethical and spiritual beliefs. The risk, if there is one, for the governors is less likely to be in forgetting the faith than in not seeing beyond it. Like other schools a faith school should work with parents and with a range of its local communities. It must deliver a broad and balanced curriculum. This includes religion, so while it will naturally prioritise its own religion it must also teach others fairly. The school serves the whole community – and is funded by public money – something that governors should bear in mind when thinking about admissions criteria and how much to prioritise adherence to the faith. They must also ensure that there is absolutely no discrimination against pupils or parents who do not subscribe to the faith.

The appointment of the chair in single academy trusts can be a delicate issue. Particularly in village church schools, the job may have gone for some time by default to the local priest. However, he or she may not be the best person to fill it. In fact, it may even be a chore for a busy priest, who ends up continuing in the post because they feel they ought to, not because they want to or are convinced that they are the right person. There may be someone else who is better equipped to do the job, and, as all governors are signed up to the school's religious ethos, there is no automatic reason why a lay person should have any less adherence to the school's core principles.

The Trust

Academy trusts have almost complete flexibility to shape their governance arrange-ments and design the constitution of their boards and local governing bodies as they see fit.

DfE, *Governors' Handbook*

The relationship of the governing body and the trust is always going to be a critical one where the two are distinct entities. Where the local governing body has few devolved responsibilities, it should not just close its eyes to those things that happen in the school for which it is not responsible. The governors will be the eyes and ears of the trust, so they should see their role as reporting to it and making recommendations. A trust with a large number of schools is not going to be able to keep a close eye on all of them, but will expect the governors to do this for them. The aim of both should be the same: to provide the best possible education for the children in the school.

When seen in this light it should be clear that the work of a local governing body is very important, even if it actual powers are sometimes limited.

Further information

C. James, S. Brammer, M. Connolly, D. Spicer, J. James & Jeff Jones, *The Chair of the School Governing Body in England: Roles, relationships and responsibilities,* (CfBT, 2013)

Martin Pounce, *Headteachers and Governing Bodies: Making the partnership work,* Adamson Publishing, 3rd edn 2013

Joan Sallis, *Parent Governors:Your own guide,* Adamson Publishing, 3rd edn 2012

Chairs of Governors' Leadership Development Programme, NCTL, www.gov.uk/school-governors-professional-development

10. Clerking

An effective clerk is vital to the success of a governing body. The evidence clearly indicates that this should be a professional role – similar to a company secretary.

House of Commons Education Committee, *The Role
of School Governing Bodies*, July 2013

There has been a growing recognition in recent years of the importance of good clerking to a governing body. Quite rightly so, because governing bodies have significant responsibilities, which they must discharge professionally, and in order to do this they need to be well run. The clerk plays an essential part, both providing the mechanism by which the governing body can function efficiently and producing the documents which are the public record of the governing body.

At one time it was thought OK for a governing body to clerk itself, but it was realised over 20 years ago that this worked against both good governance and good clerking. Since then the clerk has had to be an independent person employed to do the task, and may not be one of the governors. Only in the event of the clerk being prevented from attending a governing body meeting may a governor now take minutes. In fact, a governing body should seriously consider going a step further, and not appoint a clerk who also works in the school, as this can lead to conflicts of interest for them.

The rule is not so strict for committees, where a governor can act as clerk. But the argument that this distracts the person from contributing fully to the meeting still applies, and it is common for committees too to be clerked by someone specially appointed, often the clerk to the full governing body.

The role of the clerk in an academy fits in the same sort of pattern as that of the governors. Their role covers the same ground as that of a clerk to a maintained school governing body, but they may also be clerking the trust in which case there will be extra responsibilities. They will also find that they may be looking round for sources of training and support, instead of being able to rely on a local authority to provide them.

The clerk's functions

The function of the clerk is defined in the Articles of Association of an academy. In the DfE's model Articles for single academies there is a single paragraph purely on clerking:

The Clerk shall be appointed by the Trustees for such term, at such remuneration and upon such conditions as they may think fit; and any Clerk so appointed may be removed by them. The Clerk shall not be a Trustee or a Chief Executive Officer/Principal. Notwithstanding this Article, the Trustees may, where the Clerk fails to attend a meeting of theirs, appoint any one of their number or any other person to act as Clerk for the purposes of that meeting. The Clerk may, but need not be, the appointed company secretary of the Academy Trust. (para 81)

However, other paragraphs in the Articles mention clerks in relation to specific tasks. Between them they describe the parameters of the role:

- The clerk convenes governing body meetings.

- Three governors together can require the clerk to call a meeting.

- The clerk sends out the notice and agenda for a meeting at least seven days in advance, unless there exceptional circumstances which warrant a meeting being called at shorter notice.

- The clerk keeps minutes of meetings.

- The clerk can receive proxies for matters requiring a poll in general meetings of the academy trust.

- Anyone becoming disqualified from being a governor informs the clerk.

- If the chair or vice chair resign, they do so in writing to the clerk.

The last two points indicate the responsibility of the clerk to keep a register of members of the governing body and trust.

All these parallel the duties of clerks to maintained schools, as specified in regulations. However, they are only the bare bones of what a good clerk does.

The fuller picture

Keeping good minutes and drawing up clear agendas is not a skill that can be taken for granted, even among people who are experienced at minuting other kinds of body. To do it even half well you need to understand how the organisation operates. Whether experienced elsewhere or not, a new clerk should have induction training on the workings of governing bodies.

Minutes have to serve as a record of who was present, and of those who was a governor. They must also record what has been decided, with clear indications of the actions agreed and who will carry out each. They therefore need to be well formatted so that readers are not struggling through a thicket of sentences to find the tasks allocated to them. Minutes are also used by other people who need to know what happened in the meeting. If they could not be present, other members of the governing body or committee should be able to bring themselves up to speed from the minutes. If the meeting was that of a committee, the minutes should present a good record for the benefit of all the governors not on it, because the governing body as a whole maintains responsibility for what its committees do and for knowing what they have discussed. Matters such as monitoring pupil performance are often delegated to committees, and, while it is not necessary for all governors to be involved in detailed discussions of them, they should certainly be familiar with the whole picture.

Approved minutes are public documents, so staff members, parents and any interested members of the public should be able to access them and understand them. They will be examined by Ofsted inspectors before they visit the school and they will draw their initial conclusions on governance from them. They should therefore record not only decisions made but indicate where the governing body has provided challenge to the school's management. Being able to do all this well requires the ability to write minutes that are concise and that record decisions prominently while at the same time including enough narrative to show how those decisions were reached.

Unlike agendas, where the model Articles specify the minimum advance notice to be given, there is no prescription on how quickly draft minutes should be circulated, but the sooner they go out the better. The clerk should not allow many days to pass before writing them and sending them to the chair of the meeting for approval – nor should they allow the chair to sit on them for long before returning them for distribution.

Writing and circulating agendas and minutes are stage one of the clerk's job. Stage two is contributing to how the governing body organises its work. A good clerk will make sure that the governors have a clear plan for the year, if necessary drafting it for them. Meetings dates should be agreed for the year at the end of the previous school year, or at the latest at the beginning of the new one. The schedule will be determined by major agenda items such as approval of the budget, setting key stage targets, dates for reviewing annual policies, approval of the school development plan and reporting on staff appraisals.

One of the banes of many governors' lives is approving policies (see chapter 8). Sometimes governors make a rod for their own backs by insisting on seeing more policies than they need to or by drafting them themselves rather than requiring the senior leadership team to do it and then submit them, but even so there remain a number of policies (listed by the DfE on Gov.uk) that governors are required to agree. A good clerk will see it as their role to maintain a list of such policies, with a note of when each is due to be next reviewed and whether it is delegated to a committee or left to the full governing body.

Clerks should also see that it is clearly recorded what tasks are delegated to what committees and should draft terms of reference with the chair of governors. The DfE recommends drawing up a scheme of delegation. While the chair should ensure that all the responsibilities of the governing body are addressed each year, the clerk can provide a useful back-up, especially in giving reminders about annual tasks such as publishing a statement on the school's use of the Pupil Premium. Both paper-based planners and software programs are available to help clerks in organising the year's work and in tracking how it is distributed around committees.

Clerking professionally

This may all sound quite onerous (and an argument for paying a clerk properly should be emerging) but for a clerk to really fulfil their function, a third level of input is required. The guidance on governance regulations for maintained schools, published in January 2014, states:

> "High quality professional clerking is crucial to the effective functioning of the board. Clerking is not only about good organisation and administration, but also, and more importantly, about helping the board understand its role, functions and legal duties. This is crucial in helping the board exercise its functions expediently and confidently, so that it can stay focused on its core functions."

The regulations themselves state that "the governing body must appoint a clerk with a view to ensuring their efficient functioning and must have regard to advice from the clerk as to the nature of the governing body's functions".

While the regulations only apply to maintained schools, there is no reason why an academy should manage with a lower standard of service. On the contrary, it may well be more demanding because of the complexity of having a trust and a local governing body.

The role of a clerk is becoming more like that of the company secretary: he or she needs to be familiar with the legal framework around school governance so as to be able to give advice on procedural matters and prevent a governing body from acting outside its powers or unconstitutionally. The relevant education law and practice are substantial, and it has become more crucial that the clerk knows about them since the DfE stopped publishing its detailed *Governors' Guide to the Law*. The situation is also fast moving, and it requires work to keep up to date. To do so involves a clerk becoming familiar with the educational sections of the Gov.uk website, that of the local authority (which will contain plenty of information that is as relevant to academies as maintained schools), Ofsted's website and a selection of independent ones. It can involve being prepared to research beyond the newspaper headlines to find out if some change announced by a politician is just a proposal, a plan for something in a year's time, is coming into force immediately, or is just a reiteration of a policy that already applies. There are services available that will help with filtering information (see end of this chapter) and many local authorities offer termly briefings for clerks.

Although, as an employee of the board and not a member, the clerk should not try to influence governing body decisions or participate in discussions on matters of opinion, they must be prepared to jump in where they think that the governing body has a misunderstanding about its role or powers, or where timely advice might prevent the governors going round in circles.

Giving a governing body the support it needs is not achieved without training. The importance of this was acknowledged by the government in 2013 when it funded a new national training course for clerks. Work on the course was completed by June 2014 for delivery across the country by the regional consortia already engaged in delivering the NCTL course for chairs. The course contains four units that are delivered to all clerks, four optional units of which each participant must complete at least one, and a final review session. One of the optional units is an introduction to academies and another addresses working in multi-school settings, including multi-academy trusts. All in all the course takes about 36 hours to complete, and consists of a mixture of face-to-face sessions, online learning, group working and personal reflection.

Other courses are also available. There is an accreditation scheme for clerks run by Hampshire and the ISCG which is available through several local authorities (see www.governors.uk.com), and both GEL and the Modern Governor include modules for clerks in their online training.

Working for the trust

For the clerk who is also servicing a trust, the role is not only like that of a company secretary, serving as the company secretary may actually be written into their job description. If so, they are responsible for ensuring that the accounting officer signs the returns that have to be completed each year, including the annual accounts, and then for filing them with the EFA or other required body. A list of what has to be done each year is included in the *Academies Financial Handbook*; it covers more than five pages. The tasks include ensuring that the trust meets according to requirements, arranging and servicing the meetings, keeping a register of members, filing annual returns, and looking after legal documents such as the funding agreement and Articles of Association.

Look after your clerk

The traffic between governing body and clerk should not be all one way. If you want your clerk to support you well, you need to acknowledge that they too have needs and be prepared to respond to them.

The following list of questions will help determine how well the governing body supports its clerk:

- Did the clerk undergo induction when he or she started?

- Does the clerk have a job description? And if they work in the school, do they have a job description for clerking that is different from that of their other job?

- Is the clerk properly paid for the work he or she does?

- Is the clerk performance managed?

- Is the clerk encouraged to subscribe to support services, and does the school pay?

- Do governors (especially chairs of committees and the governing body) respond quickly to communications from the clerk?

- Is the clerk encouraged to take on administrative tasks?

Even if the clerk has experience of working for other schools, as a new clerk he or she cannot be expected to hit the ground running. A new clerk needs to be introduced to the school and to meet key staff, and to be told who the governors are and what the meeting arrangements are. There are various documents about the school and the governing body that should be supplied from the outset, not least:

- a clear written job description

- a letter of appointment giving appointment start date

- a contract of appointment (statement of particulars) within eight weeks of the commencement date

- the induction pack given to new governors

- up-to-date records relating to the governing body, such as their appointment dates, contact details and committee membership.

Recognising that it is a paid job means that it should be properly remunerated; the local governor services department can probably provide a going rate for your area.

"Performance management" might sound like too formal a term for someone whose job is part time, and it is certainly not recommended to set up a process similar to the appraisal of a principal. But the chair or vice chair ought to sit down with the clerk annually and discuss how the job is going, and what mutual expectations are. This should be for the benefit of both parties, giving the clerk the opportunity to raise any problems of their own as well as letting the governing body comment on practice. It is a part of being treated as a professional.

Further information

Clerkwise, www.adamsonbooks.com. An online subscription service for clerks to governing bodies that contains tools for clerks, documents giving guidance on governing body responsibilities, models for statutory policies, and a twice-termly newsletter written specially for clerks.

GEL (Governors' e-Learning), www.elc-gel.org, and Modern Governor, www.moderngovernor.com, are suppliers of online training for governors, and include training modules for clerks. GEL also carries some good practice documents.

The Governors Virtual Office, www.schoolleadershipsystems.com – a web-based tool that helps governing bodies organise and manage their work.

Hampshire Governor Services and Information for School and College Governors (ISCG) run an accreditation scheme for clerks, the Accredited Clerk, which is delivered by a number of local authorities.

11. Terminology and Abbreviations

APPG	*All Party Parliamentary Group; in the context of governance usually refers to the APPG on Education, Governance and Leadership*
Articles of Association	*document that determines an organisation's constitution: the roles and powers of directors, the business it undertakes, and how members or shareholders appoint and dismiss directors.*
ASCL	*Association of School and College Leaders*
ATL	*Association of Teachers and Lecturers*
AWPU or AWPA	*Age-Weighted Pupil Unit or Age Weighted Pupil Allocation – unit used in calculating the funding of the school, weighted according to the pupils' ages.*
BME/BAME	*Black and minority ethnic*
BTEC	*Business and Technology Education Council – name also given to the qualifications it awards for vocational courses*
Cohort	*Body of pupils entering a school in any one year*
CPD	*Continuing Professional Development*
DBS	*Disclosure and Barring Service*
DfE	*Department for Education*
EAL	*English as an Additional Language*
EBac/EBacc	*English Baccalaureate, which pupils are deemed to have achieved if they gain A*–C GCSEs in English, maths, geography or history, two sciences and a foreign language*
EFA	*Education Funding Agency – body responsible for the funding of academies, Free Schools and 16-19 provision*
EHC plan	*Education and Health Care plan – support for children with pronounced Special Educational Need*
ESG	*Education Services Grant. Grant paid to both academies and local authorities to cover services that local authorities provide centrally for maintained schools*
Estyn	*Inspection body for education and training in Wales*
FE	*Further Education*
FMGS	*Financial Management and Governance Self-assessment – a self assessment tool and statement to check a new academy is following good financial practice*
FTE	*Full Time Equivalent – part-time staff measured according*

to how many full-time staff would be required to work the same number of hours

Funding agreement *The contract to set up an academy, which defines the obligations of the company setting up the academy and of the government to support it financially*

GAG	*General Annual Grant – annual funding for an academy*
G&T	*Gifted and talented*
HE	*Higher Education*
HMCI	*Her Majesty's Chief Inspector – the head of Ofsted*
HMI	*Her Majesty's Inspector*
ICT	*Information and Communications Technology*
IEB	*Interim Executive Board. Temporary board of governors appointed to replace the governing body of a failing school*
IEP	*Individual Education Plan*
INSET	*In-Service Training for Teachers*
ITT	*Initial Teacher Training*
KS1(2/3/4)	*Key Stage One (Two/Three/Four). The term Key Stage Five is sometimes used to describe the sixth form level.*
LA	*Local Authority*
LADO	*Local Authority Designated Officer – to whom child protection cases involving allegations against school staff and volunteers must be referred*
LSA	*Learning Support Assistant*
MAT	*Multi-academy trust*
MLD	*Moderate Learning Difficulties*
NAHT	*National Association of Head Teachers*
NASEN	*National Association for Special Educational Needs*
NASUWT	*National Association of Schoolmasters/Union of Women Teachers*
NCTL	*The National College for Teaching and Leadership (part of the DfE)*
NEET	*Not in education, employment or training*
NGA	*National Governors' Association*
NLE	*National Leader of Education*
NLG	*National Leader of Governance – an experienced and skilled governor available to help governing bodies*
NPQH	*National Professional Qualification for Headship*
NQT	*Newly Qualified Teacher*
NUT	*National Union of Teachers*
NVQ	*National Vocational Qualification*

Ofqual	*Office of the Qualifications and Examinations Regulator*
Ofsted	*Office for Standards in Education, Children's Services and Skills*
PAN	*Published admission number - the maximum number (with some exceptions) of new pupils that a school will admit in a an age group*
PPA	*Preparation, planning and assessment time – designated non-teaching time for teachers*
PRU	*Pupil Referral Unit*
PSA	*Parent Support Adviser*
PSHE	*Personal, Social and Health Education*
PTA	*Parent Teacher Association*
PTA-UK	*National association for PTAs*
Pupil Premium	*Grant paid to all schools based on the number of pupils in the school eligible for free school meals, to be used by the school to boost the achievement of pupils from disadvantaged backgrounds.*
QTS	*Qualified Teacher Status*
RAISEonline	*Reporting and Analysis for Improvement through School Self-Evaluation. On-line data on pupil performance for each school published by Ofsted and DfE*
SACRE	*Standing Advisory Council for Religious Education – body which advises on religious education and worship*
SATs	*Standard Assessment Tests – commonly used (though unofficial) name for national tests carried out in England at ages 7 and 14*
SD/IP	*School Development/Improvement Plan*
SEAL	*Social and Emotional Aspects of Learning*
SEN	*Special Educational Needs*
SENCO	*Special Educational Needs Co-ordinator*
SEND	*Special Educational Needs and Disabilities*
SGOSS	*Used to stand for School Governors' One-Stop Shop, now simply the initials – organisation that recruits people interested in becoming governors*
SLT	*Senior Leadership Team*
SMSC	*Spiritual, Moral, Social and Cultural*
SORP	*Statement of Recommended Practice – in the case of charities (and hence academies) a framework of recommended practice for accounting and reporting*
STRB	*School Teachers' Review Body – group that advises the government on teachers' pay and conditions in maintained schools each year*
TA	*Teaching assistant*
TLR	*Teaching and Learning Responsibility – management responsibility for which a teacher receives extra pay*
TUPE	*Transfer of Undertakings (Protection of Employment) regulations*

UCAS	*Universities and Colleges Admissions Service*
UTC	*University Technical College*
VA	*Voluntary Aided*
VC	*Voluntary Controlled*

12. Sources of Information

Details of documents referred to in the text are given in the relevant chapters. The following lists other useful documents (both paper and electronically published) on topics covered in this book.

Government departments are referred to by their name at the time of publication, e.g. DfE after June 2010, DCSF before June 2010.

General roles

Governors' Handbook, DfE, only available online at www.gov.uk

Being Strategic, David Marriott, Adamson Publishing, 3rd edn 2011

GEL (Governors' E-Learning), www.elc-gel.org, on-line training for governors

Modern Governor, www.moderngovernor.com, on-line training for governors

The Governor, www.thegovernor.org.uk, website for school governors containing news and useful documents

General information on academies is available from the Department for Education on the government's website, www.gov.uk.

FAQs for those considering taking on academy status are on the Academies pages of the Department for Education's section of www.gov.uk. Regularly updated advice for governors on converting to an academy is also available for NGA members on its website, www.nga.org.uk

Unleashing Greatness: Getting the best from an academised system, Academies Commission, RSA, www.thersa.org>Action and research>Learning, cognition and creativity>Education

Admissions

School Admissions Code, DfE, www.gov.uk

Appointing and recruiting staff

A Guide to Recruiting and Selecting a New Headteacher, National College in conjunction with the National Governors' Association, www.nga. org.uk

Training in Safer Recruitment and FAQs about Safer Recruitment Training, DfE, www.gov.uk

Recruiting Headteachers and Senior Leaders, National College for Leadership of Schools and Children's Services, www.gov.uk

Appraisal

Knowing Your School: Governors and Staff Performance, NGA & NCOGS, www.nga.org.uk/Resources/Knowing-Your-School.aspx

Teacher Appraisal and Capability – A model policy for schools, DfE, www.gov.uk. These pages also give guidance.

Bullying

Bullying at School, DfE, www.gov.uk

No Place for Bullying, Ofsted, www.ofsted.gov.uk/resources/no-place-for-bullying

Careers advice

Careers Guidance and Inspiration in Schools: Departmental advice for governing bodies, school leaders and school staff, DfE, www.gov.uk

Chairing

Leading Governors, NGA and National College, www.gov.uk/government/publications/leading-governors-the-role-of-the-chair-of-governors

The National College pages of www.gov.uk contain other useful resources for chairs.

Information on the Chairs of Governors' Leadership Development Programme is on www.gov.uk under "School governors: professional development"

Charging and school visits

Charging for School Activities: Departmental advice for governing bodies, school leaders, school staff and local authorities, DfE, www.gov.uk

Charitable status

The Charity Commission, www.charitycommission.gov.uk, has details of your obligations as a charity and advice on trusteeship. You can file your annual returns here.

Child protection
Various documents are published on the DfE section of www.gov.uk.

Clerking
Clerkwise, regularly updated on-line information service for clerks, www.adamsonbooks.com

Manual for Governing Bodies and their Clerks, 14th edn, ISCG, 2013

Governors Virtual Office, www.schoolleadershipsystems.com, on-line tool to manage the governing body's work and communications

For Clerks, section of the GEL website (*see* GENERAL ROLES)

Complaints
School Complaints Toolkit 2015: Departmental advice for maintained schools, maintained nursery schools and local authorities, DfE, www.gov.uk

Countering terrorism and radicalism
The Prevent Duty: departmental advice for schools and childcare providers, DfE, www.gov.uk

Curriculum
The DfE section of www.gov.uk gives details of the curriculum for both maintained schools and academies, including the National Curriculum

Promoting Fundamental British Values as Part of SMSC in Schools: departmental advice for maintained schools, DfE, www.gov.uk

Data
Knowing Your School, Primary RAISEonline, RM Education and NGA, NGA, 2014

Knowing Your School, Secondary RAISEonline, RM Education and NGA, NGA, 2014

Fischer Family Trust, www.fft.org.uk. The FFT Governor Dashboard can be downloaded by subscribing schools, while anyone can download a model and a guide as to how to use it from the same site (www.fft.org.uk/fft-live/about-FFT-Live.aspx).

FFT Aspire, on the same website, is a reporting and data tool for schools

RAISEonline, www.raiseonline.org

School Data Dashboards (Ofsted) for all schools are on http://dashboard.ofsted.gov.uk

Disability
Disability Discrimination Act Code of Practice for Schools,
www.equalityhumanrights.com/advice-and-guidance/information-for-advisers/codes-of-practice

Drugs
DfE and ACPO Drug Advice for Schools, DfE, 2012, www.gov.uk

Equality
Education Providers: Schools Guidance, Equality and Human Rights Commission, www.equalityhumanrights.com>Advice and guidance

Exclusions
Exclusions from Maintained Schools, Academies and Pupil Referral Units in England: a guide for those with legal responsibility in relation to exclusion, DfE, www.gov.uk

Finance
Financial documents are on the DfE section of www.gov.uk in the Statutory Guidance and DfE Advice sections, both under the heading Administration and Finance. The former includes *Schemes for Financing Schools* and the latter *Effective Buying for Your School*

Guidance from the Education Funding Agency on the funding of academies and the use of financial resources, including the *Academies Financial Handbook*, are on www.gov.uk, under "Academies: funding, payments and compliance"

Companies House: www.companieshouse.org.uk – the address for filing annual returns and company accounts.

Free Schools
New Schools Network, www.newschoolsnetwork.org. Gives advice to potential suppliers of new schools

Freedom of Information
The Information Commissioner, www.informationcommissioner.gov.uk Guidance on the application of the Freedom of Information Act

Governing body improvement
School Governance: Learning from the best, Ofsted 2011

All Party Parliamentary Group on Education, Governance and Leadership, *Twenty Key Questions for a School Governing Body to Ask Itself* and *Twenty-One Questions for Multi-Academy Trusts*, www.nga.org.uk

Various documents are on the NGA's website, under "Improving your governing board", www.nga.org.uk

Governing body succession
Succession Breeds Success: How to grow leaders in your governing body, National Co-ordinators of Governor Services, www.ncogs.org.uk

Health and safety
Departmental Advice on Health and Safety for Schools, DfE, www.gov.uk

Inspection
School Self-Evaluation, Improvement and Inspection: A practical guide for school governors, Martin Pounce, Adamson Publishing, 2012

Ofsted, *Common Inspection: education, skills and early years,* www.gov.uk

Ofsted, *School Inspection Handbook*, www.gov.uk

Insurance
Academies Risk Protection Arrangement (RPA), www.gov.uk. An alternative to insurance for academies, where losses that arise are covered by UK government funds

Looked after children
Various documents can be found on the DfE section of www.gov.uk under "Looked-after children"

Monitoring
Monitoring and Evaluation: A practical guide for school governors, David Marriott, Adamson Publishing, 3rd edn, 2011

New governors
Start Here: A guide for new governors, Adamson Publishing, rev. edn 2013

Welcome to Governance, NGA

Parent governors

Parent Governors: Your own guide, Joan Sallis, Adamson Publishing, 2012

Parents

Effective Partnerships with Parents (EPPa) Toolkit, Southgate Publishers www.southgatepublishers.co.uk

Information and guidance on many aspects of parenting, including school admissions, bullying and becoming a governor, are on www.gov.uk

Parent View, section of the Ofsted website where parents can answer a 12-question survey on their views of their child's school, http://parentview.ofsted.gov.uk

PE and Sport Premium

A Guide for Governors: Maximising the impact of the primary PE and sport funding, Youth Sport Trust, www.youthsporttrust.org

The Youth Sport Trust also provides support on using the premium on its website

Performance management

See APPRAISAL

Planning

Being Strategic: A practical guide for school governors and headteachers, David Marriott, Adamson Publishing, rev. edn 2011

Policies

Statutory Policies for Schools, DfE, www.gov.uk

Principals and governors

Headteachers and Governing Bodies: A practical guide to making the partnership work, Martin Pounce, Adamson Publishing, rev. edn 2013

What Governing Boards Should Expect from School Leaders and What School Leaders Should Expect from Governing Boards, NGA, NAHT, ASCL and LGA, revised edition 2015, available to members on the NGA website (www.nga.org.uk)

Procurement

Review of Efficiency in the Schools System, DfE, www.gov.uk

Efficiency Toolkit for Schools, Education Funding Agency, online support for academies on how to spend money efficiently, www.gov.uk

The Crown Commercial Service, a department of the Cabinet Office, publishes a quarterly *Schools and Academies Newsletter*, giving information on meeting the regulations surrounding how public money is spent and helping schools achieve best value, www.gov.uk

Pupil behaviour
Various documents, including *Behaviour and Discipline in Schools*, can be found on the DfE section of www.gov.uk

Pupil Premium
DfE, *Evaluation of Pupil Premium*, www.gov.uk>Publications

DfE, *Pupil Premium: Funding and accountability for schools*, www.gov.uk

Ofsted, *The Pupil Premium: Analysis and challenge tools for schools*, www.gov.uk

Sutton Trust/Education Endowment Foundation, *Teaching and Learning Toolkit*, gives research-based guidance on how successfully a wide range of initiatives work in practice to improve the attainment of disadvantaged pupils, https://educationendowmentfoundation.org.uk/toolkit/

Pupil voice
Children's Commissioner for England, www.childrenscommissioner.gov.uk

School Councils UK, www.schoolcouncils.org

Recruitment of governors
SGOSS, www.sgoss.org.uk, finds and holds lists of people wishing to become governors, and gives advice on governor recruitment

Inspiring Governors, www.inspiringgovernors.org, has a database of people with professional backgrounds looking to volunteer, including as school governors

Recruitment of staff
See APPOINTING AND RECRUITING STAFF

Religious education
Religious education in English schools: Non-statutory guidance 2010, DfE, www.gov.uk

Safeguarding

Disclosure and Barring Service, www.gov.uk

Keeping Children Safe in Education (statutory guidance), DfE, www.gov.uk

See also CHILD PROTECTION

School self-evaluation

School Self-Evaluation, Improvement and Inspection: A practical guide for school governors, Martin Pounce, Adamson Publishing, 2012

Special Educational Needs and Disability

The DfE section of www.gov.uk contains a range of documents, including the *SEND Code of Practice: 0 to 25 years* and *Schools: Guide to the 0 to 25 SEND code of practice*

NASEN, www.nasen.org.uk, has guidance on SEN for its members

Succession planning

NCOGS, *Succession Breeds Success*, rev. edn 2014, www.ncogs.org.uk/ resources.php

Teachers' pay

Under "School teachers' pay and conditions: advice", www.gov.uk, the DfE provides guidance documents on implementing a school's pay policy and HR practice in relation to pay

School Teachers' Pay and Conditions Document, on the DfE section of www.gov.uk

Terrorism

See COUNTERING TERRORISM AND RADICALISM

Index